'*The Architect and the Academy* encapsul
the eminent career of Dean Hawkes, a tri
practice – whether tectonic-musical 'play' between Alvar Aalto and Joonas
Kokkonen, or career-comparisons of Leslie Martin and Serge Chermayeff.
Hence Hawkes' essays bring compulsive fascination and intrigue to the
"environmental dimension of architecture".'

Colin Porteous, *Emeritus Professor, The*
Glasgow School of Art, UK

'Dean Hawkes' career connecting architectural research, practice, writing
and teaching has spanned fifty years. His new book collects reflections on
architectural research culture and environmental and technical imagination.
Hawkes's essays demonstrate that environmental theories and histories –
increasingly popular and urgent because of our climate crisis – are not new
but extend from long-standing disciplinary values and habits.'

Adam Sharr, *Professor of Architecture, and*
Head of the School of Architecture, Planning
and Landscape, at Newcastle University, UK

'Drawing from essays written across his long career, Hawkes establishes
design as the proper mode of inquiry in architecture, distinguishing it from
the kinds of research conducted in the sciences and humanities from which
it necessarily borrows. He explores similar approaches by Renaissance and
contemporary architects, for whom experiments with light, sound, and heat
are methods of discovery and invention.'

William W. Braham, FAIA, *Professor &*
Director, Department of Architecture,
Weitzman School of Design, University of
Pennsylvania, USA

'These Dean Hawkes' reflections become a fundamental book for understanding a fundamental moment in the evolution of architecture.'

Sergio Los, *Professor of Architectural*
Composition, IUAV University
of Venice, Italy

'Dean Hawkes' books never fail to delight and to inspire, and this one is no
exception. It is both thoughtful and thought-provoking, beautifully evocative
and simultaneously rigorous in its historical and factual approach. This is a
book to be read slowly and savoured as the themes of each essay unfold. It
deftly establishes the positioning of architecture within the academy and the
manner in which different disciplines and the strands of education, research
and practice were woven together – with different degrees of tension – to
shape that positioning.'

Fiona Smyth, *Trinity College Dublin, Ireland*

The Architect and the Academy

This book presents an expansive overview of the development of architectural and environmental research, with authoritative essays spanning Dean Hawkes' impressive 50-year academic career.

The book considers the relationship between the technologies of the environment and wider historical and theoretical factors, with chapters on topics ranging from the origins of modern 'building science' in Renaissance England to technology and imagination in architecture. It includes numerous architectural examples from renowned architects such as Christopher Wren, Peter Zumthor, Alvar Aalto, Robert Venturi and Carlo Scarpa.

Aimed at students, scholars, and researchers in architecture and beyond, this illustrated volume collates important and wide-ranging essays tracing the definition, scope and methodologies of architectural and environmental studies, with a foreword by Susannah Hagan.

Dean Hawkes has been a teacher, researcher and practitioner of architecture for over half a century. For 30 years he taught and researched in the Department of Architecture at the University of Cambridge and, between 1995 and 2002, was professor of architectural design at the Welsh School of Architecture at Cardiff University. Following his retirement, he returned to Cambridge as a fellow of Darwin College, where he continues to research and teach. He retired from architectural practice in 2010. His research focusses on the relationship between *technics* and *poetics* in architecture and is principally concerned with questions of environmental design. The essays collected in this book range across this broad field, covering two distinct themes: *The Culture and Origins of Architectural Research* and *Themes in the Architecture of Environment*. Together these complement the author's series of Routledge books: *The Environmental Tradition* (1996), *The Selective Environment* (2001), *The Environmental Imagination* (1st ed. 2008, 2nd ed. 2019) and *Architecture and Climate* (2012).

Routledge Research in Architecture

The *Routledge Research in Architecture* series provides the reader with the latest scholarship in the field of architecture. The series publishes research from across the globe and covers areas as diverse as architectural history and theory, technology, digital architecture, structures, materials, details, design, monographs of architects, interior design and much more. By making these studies available to the worldwide academic community, the series aims to promote quality architectural research.

Cybernetic Architectures
Informational Thinking and Digital Design
Camilo Andrés Cifuentes Quin

Jørn Utzon and Transcultural Essentialism
Adrian Carter and Marja Sarvimäki

Husserl and Spatiality
Toward a Phenomenological Ethnography of Space
Tao DuFour

Radical Functionalism
A Social Architecture for Mexico
Luis E. Carranza

The Architect and the Academy
Essays on Research and Environment
Dean Hawkes

Architecture of Threshold Spaces
A Critique of the Ideologies of Hyperconnectivity and Segregation in the Socio-Political Context
Laurence Kimmel

For more information about this series, please visit: https://www.routledge
.com/Routledge-Research-in-Architecture/book-series/RRARCH

The Architect and the Academy

Essays on Research and Environment

Dean Hawkes

Foreword by Susannah Hagan

Routledge
Taylor & Francis Group

LONDON AND NEW YORK

Cover image: Villa Kokkonen, by Alvar Aalto, Interior detail. Photograph by Dean Hawkes.

First published 2022
by Routledge
2 Park Square, Milton Park, Abingdon, Oxon OX14 4RN

and by Routledge
605 Third Avenue, New York, NY 10158

Routledge is an imprint of the Taylor & Francis Group, an informa business

British Library Cataloguing-in-Publication Data
A catalogue record for this book is available from the British Library

Library of Congress Cataloging-in-Publication Data
Names: Hawkes, Dean, author. | Hagan, Susannah, writer of foreword.
Title: The architect and the academy: essays on research and environment/Dean Hawkes; foreword by Susannah Hagan.
Description: Abingdon, Oxon; New York, NY: Routledge, 2022. |
Series: Routledge research in architecture | Includes bibliographical references and index.
Identifiers: LCCN 2021033478 (print) | LCCN 2021033479 (ebook) |
ISBN 9780367537159 (hardback) | ISBN 9780367537166 (paperback) |
ISBN 9781003083023 (ebook)
Subjects: LCSH: Architecture–Research. | Buildings–Environmental engineering–Research.
Classification: LCC NA2005 .H39 2022 (print) | LCC NA2005 (ebook) |
DDC 720.72–dc23
LC record available at https://lccn.loc.gov/2021033478
LC ebook record available at https://lccn.loc.gov/2021033479

ISBN: 978-0-367-53715-9 (hbk)
ISBN: 978-0-367-53716-6 (pbk)
ISBN: 978-1-003-08302-3 (ebk)

DOI: 10.4324/9781003083023

Typeset in Sabon
by Deanta Global Publishing Services, Chennai, India

Contents

Figures

Foreword

Susannah Hagan

The tradition of the architectural practitioner–writer is a rich seam in architectural scholarship and ran through the second half of the twentieth century in the writings of architects such as Alan Colquhoun, Robert Maxwell and Colin St John Wilson, among others. They had in common a view of architecture as its own subject, with its own imperatives driven by social and tectonic ideas. The wholesale importation of theory from other disciplines in the 1980s and 90s, most notably Deconstruction from philosophy and complexity from physics, introduced a different way of thinking about architecture: as a subject within a larger theoretical framework. This decentring of architecture had happened before, in the 1970s, in Marxist analysis by writers like Manfredo Tafuri, but Marxism was a very different kind of meta-narrative, being concerned with economics and distributions of power that drive architecture as much as any other undertaking in the world.

The turn to theories like Deconstruction threatened to divide architectural writing from architectural practice and production and their urgent needs. But at the same time that such extra-architectural frameworks were having their effect upon the academy, the social sciences were making a considerable contribution to architecture in-the-world: first to thinking on the city – who makes it and who has access to it – and second to thinking on 'agency' – the roles of the professional and the public in producing the built environment, encouraging a return to architecture as a means to analysing and understanding architecture. Dean Hawkes' writings are a testament to this approach, and a continuation of the practitioner–writer tradition.

There were two prods to a greater appreciation of evidence-based writing: the first was the erosion, beginning in the early 1990s, of the architect's leadership of the production of buildings, and the need to understand its causes. The second was the increasing uneasiness about a biosphere less and less able to absorb the impact of our actions on it and the importance of understanding architecture's role in that impact. That some version of architectural leadership could be reconstituted by joining the two concerns, with architects leading an environmental reformation, is only just dawning on most in the profession. A few, like Dean Hawkes, have been championing it since the 1960s.

What sets him apart from his generation of architectural writers, and from most other architectural writers for that matter, is his ability to integrate what he refers to as the poetics of architecture with environmental technics. This has been a life's work, combining the design of architecture with the study of architectural composition and the analysis of environmental performance as a result of that composition. Hawkes, the designer contains Hawkes, the historian and Hawkes, the environmental pioneer. This work is represented in the second half of *The Architect and the Academy*, in essays that combine a forensic eye for detail with a phenomenological appreciation of design. They are part of the thinking that gave rise to earlier books of his, like *The Environmental Tradition* and *The Environmental Imagination*, though with the addition of musical comparisons that are as enriching as they are unexpected. This writing asks what a building feels like. What is the quality of its light? Its temperature? Its materials? How has this design created the particular 'it-ness' of this object? For Hawkes, the environment is part of architectural culture, and architectural culture, part of the environment.

In contrast, the essays in the first half of this book examine the context out of which the content of Hawkes' thinking has developed over the years. This is a geographical and intellectual context that he is singularly well-placed to discuss, having been a young architect academic at Cambridge University during the extraordinary flowering of architectural research in the 1960s and 70s under Leslie Martin – and during the decades after. The book's first four essays examine the debates in the UK and the US about the nature and production of architectural research in the mid-twentieth century. In these, research, and emphatically design research, was held up as the *sine qua non* of both architectural education and the constituting of architecture as a discipline.

These debates raise now, as they raised then, some fascinating questions: What is the position of practice within a discipline? Can there be a discipline without research? What constitutes the research of the discipline of architecture? What are the alternatives to the scientific method? Environmental design has made this last question as pertinent today as it was then. Then, the dividing line was the acceptance or rejection of what Philip Steadman at Cambridge in 1979 called the 'distinction between the objective and analytical character of science and the value-laden subjective and synthetic character of design'. Within the environmental problematic, Hawkes has shown us it is entirely possible to integrate these rather than choose between them. For him, 'It is the function of the academic in architecture to conduct a continuing critique of the state of practice'. This, as an academic and a practitioner, he has done throughout his life with erudition and humanity and does so again in this book.

Acknowledgements

I have worked on this book in the period between spring 2020 and summer 2021, when the world has suffered the restrictions that followed the global outbreak of Covid-19. Because the content is based on a group of previously published essays and conference presentations, it has been possible to carry out most of the new work using material from my personal library and the vast resources accessible through the internet. The process has been quite unlike the research for my two previous books, *The Environmental Imagination* (2008 & 2020) and *Architecture and Climate* (2012). Each of those was based on extensive field studies, in which I visited the buildings that constituted the core of the research. This necessitated travel far and wide in Britain, Europe and North America, as I sought direct experience of these remarkable places. This would, of course, have been impossible under the pandemic. In its place I have walked most days to the study in the garden of my house in Cambridge.

Nonetheless, I have received help from many, who I should like to thank. The holders of copyright on the original publication of the essays have generously given permission to produce these revised versions and are individually acknowledged at the end of each essay. I have also been given permission to reproduce images from many sources and these are acknowledged in the List of Figures. I should like to give particular thanks to the practising architects who have unfailingly and swiftly provided images, photographs and drawings of their buildings at a time when maintaining their professional work must be difficult. On the academic front, the essays would not have been written in their original form if I had not received invitations to contribute to conferences and seminars. I am grateful to all those who have so kindly given me these opportunities.

Finally, my thanks go to my editors at Routledge, Fran Ford and Trudy Varcianna, who have been consistently helpful and supportive.

Dean Hawkes,
Cambridge,
2021.

Introduction

> The advancement of knowledge is not merely an ornament to a profession – it is its duty. This is the means by which the competence of the profession as a whole can be advanced. It is essential to improvement in both teaching and practice that a limited number of people should at some time devote themselves to advanced post-graduate study and research.
>
> *– Leslie Martin, 1958*

The modern origins of research in architecture in Britain may be traced to the Conference on Architectural Education that was organised by the Royal Institute of British Architects and held at Magdalen College, Oxford, from 11th to 13th April 1958. The statement above is drawn from the report on the conference that was published in the *RIBA Journal* in June 1958.[1] The conference was chaired by Leslie Martin, the head of the school of architecture at the University of Cambridge, who was also the author of the anonymous report. In 1965 I had the good fortune to join the Cambridge school as a very junior research assistant to work on studies of daylighting in relation to the design of mass housing. I remained at the school, teaching in both the lecture room and the design studio, and researching, until 1995, when I moved to the Welsh School of Architecture at Cardiff University as professor of architectural design. In 2002, I returned to Cambridge to rejoin Darwin College as a fellow and to work from my study in the garden of the house that I had designed and built in the city in 1991. Over those years I consistently engaged in architectural practice in some measure, until I closed my last, small office in 2010.

This is the background to the essays in this book that are drawn from publications and conference papers that first appeared over a period of 25 years. These derive from my activity in academic research, and the majority relate to my principal interest in the environmental dimension of architecture. To these I have added an introductory group that addresses questions regarding modern research in architecture, first, of its nature and conduct and, second, of its history. Over the years I have reflected on these broader matters from my standpoint as researcher, teacher and practitioner, and my hope in including these essays is to add a little to the ongoing debate

DOI: 10.4324/9781003083023-1

on the definition of architectural research and, in particular, the question of design as research. The title of the book is taken from the second of these essays and, although that is concerned with the work of specific and significant practitioner–teachers of the twentieth century, I intend it also to express something of my own perspective as an architect who has spent a lifetime *in* the academy.

The nature and practice of architectural research

The first pair of essays are concerned with the definition and methodology of research in architecture. 'The centre and the periphery: Some reflections on the nature and conduct of research in architecture', is based on a talk given to the Martin Centre Research Society at Cambridge in October 1994. It was conceived as a reflection on the experience of the 30 years I had then spent researching and teaching at the Cambridge school, and argues that research should embrace both the architectural humanities and architectural science and that, crucially, a place should be found for design as a legitimate *mode of enquiry* in architecture – that design *is* research. It examines the continuing relevance of the model of architectural research which was proposed at the Oxford Conference. It suggests that the 'Oxford Model', with its roots in the procedures of the sciences, in which 'fundamental' research preceded 'development' before leading into practical application, fails to account for developments in the scope and methods of architectural research in the years following the conference and, importantly, disregards the role of design as a mode of architectural enquiry. It also proposes that developments in architectural education, in particular the growth of the unit system of studio instruction, have added a further element to the productive and investigative potential of the schools of architecture, and that this should be accounted for in any valid model of research.

The second essay, 'The architect and the academy', follows on from 'The centre and the periphery' to develop further the proposition that design practice, both in its processes and products, constitutes the core, the *centre*, of the discipline of architecture and goes on to examine the implications of this for the form, content and delivery of architectural education. The argument is illustrated by outlines of the ideas of a quartet of distinguished practitioner–teachers: Herman Herzberger, Louis Kahn, Carlo Scarpa and Peter Zumthor. Using accounts of their respective pedagogies, the essay seeks to show something of the unique insights into the nature of architecture that practitioners alone may convey within the education process.

These introductory essays are followed by a second pair that is concerned specifically with the origins of research at the Cambridge school of architecture in the 1960s. The first, 'The shaping of architectural research: Transatlantic transactions', draws a comparison between Leslie Martin's objectives at the British Cambridge and those of Serge Chermayeff at the Graduate School of Design at Harvard in the 'other' Cambridge

(Massachusetts). In the 2020s it is axiomatic that most, if not all, faculty members of schools of architecture will undertake some measure of research. In this the academic architect stands alongside and is indistinguishable from colleagues in other disciplines. But in the middle decades of the last century, the case for the development of a research culture in architecture was not so clear-cut. This essay describes how Martin and Chermayeff set about establishing research in the parallel but, in many ways, distinct contexts of their respective academic and architectural cultures.

The final essay in the first part, 'Bridging the cultures: Architecture, models and computers in 1960s Cambridge', looks in detail at the early years of organised research in Cambridge, UK, where, under the direction of Leslie Martin, a unique research centre was founded in the Department of Architecture. Before that date, research in architecture was fragmentary and consisted largely of individual studies of topics in architectural history. In the newly established centre for Land Use and Built Form Studies, a group of young researchers, all, not insignificantly, architecture graduates, embarked on a programme of research. Informed by an interest in the idea of the 'model' that was prevalent across disciplines in Cambridge at this time, from Economics, Archaeology, Geography and to the History and Philosophy of Science, and by using the power of the University Mathematical Laboratory's 'Titan' mainframe computer, the group developed conceptual and mathematical models that operated across the range of architectural scales from building to city. This essay describes that work and sets it in the context of Martin's wider role in reshaping architectural education in Britain.

Themes in the architecture of environment

The first essay in the second part of the book, 'The environment of the Elizabethan house: Hardwick Hall', is a study of this remarkable building that was built between 1591 and 1597 and is one of the most important houses of Elizabethan England. It was the home of Elizabeth, Countess of Shrewsbury and the work of the architect Robert Smythson. I first discussed Hardwick in the Introduction to my book, *The Environmental Imagination*,[2] where I drew a comparison between it and Palladio's near contemporary Villa Capra, La Rotonda, as both evincing deep understanding of the implications of climate, of Derbyshire and the Veneto respectively, in their form, materiality and detail. This study of Hardwick shows how the exterior observes and dramatically demonstrates the principles of strict symmetry that were an important aspect of the architecture of the English renaissance and how this conceals a surprising asymmetry and complexity of internal organisation. Examination of the plans shows how this organisation is founded on the observation of what we now recognise to be the principles of environmental design. The essay constructs a description of the environment of the house as it might have been experienced when it was first occupied at the end of the sixteenth century.

Robert Smythson also plays a part in the essay that follows, 'The origins of building science in the architecture of Renaissance England'. This examines how architecture was transformed by the emergence of organised science in England in the period between the end of the sixteenth century and the middle years of the eighteenth century. The discussion is principally concerned with the aspect of building design that we now identify as 'environmental' and focusses on three distinct phases in architectural history; the last years of the reign of Queen Elizabeth I, with the remarkable 'prodigy' houses built by Smythson and others; the second half of the seventeenth century, when Christopher Wren, both scientist and architect, emerged as the dominant figure in English architecture; and the middle years of the eighteenth century when the 'Palladian' movement adopted and adapted the sixteenth-century architecture of the Veneto to the English condition. Through these phases the 'science' of architecture is shown to advance from the numberless precision of Smythson's environmental strategies, through the connection between Wren's engagement with the science of meteorology and the environments of his buildings, to the influence of Isaac Newton on the environmental tabulations of the seventeenth century theoretician, Robert Morris, and their relation to the designs of the English Palladians.

'Imagining Light: the measureable and the unmeasureable of daylight design', focusses specifically on daylight in buildings. The art of daylighting involves much more than merely achieving appropriate quantities of natural light into a building. Acts of great architectural imagination may transform the utilitarian functions of daylighting – *the measureable* – into places of great beauty – *the unmeasureable* – in the terminology proposed by Louis Kahn.[3] The essay begins with a study of the masterly illumination of the interior of Christopher Wren's church of St. Stephen Walbrook, before proceeding to a comparative study of daylight in Sir John Soane's house and museum at Lincoln's Inn Fields, London and Carlo Scarpa's extension to the Museo Canoviano at Possagno. The possibilities of daylight in 'buildings for all purposes' are presented in descriptions of twentieth-century designs by Louis Kahn, at the Yale Center for British Art at New Haven, Peter Zumthor in the Shelter for Roman Remains at Chur, in the Heelis office building in Swindon by the British practice FCBS and a small house in Cambridge by the author.

The term 'selective environment' defines an approach to environmentally responsive architectural design in which connections are made between the technical preoccupations of architectural science and the necessity to sustain cultural identity in the face of rapid global change. The essay, 'The selective environment: Environmental design and cultural identity', summarises the fundamentals of selective design theory, with particular emphasis on the themes of 'environment and regionalism', 'nature and architecture' and the relation of 'comfort and climate', as these are laid out in the writings of Kenneth Frampton, Victor Olgyay, Alexander Tzonis and Lianne Lefaivre, and the author and colleagues.[4] The method proposes the importance of historical analysis in shaping contemporary design practice and building technology. The aim is to develop an alternative, climate responsive and culturally grounded basis for design in the twenty-first century in opposition to the universal strategy of the sealed building envelope enclosing artificial environments delivered by mechanical plant.

In 'The Technical Imagination: thoughts on the relation of technique and design in architecture', the aim is to show that decisions about material, structure, construction and environmental services in architecture are not exclusively matters of technical, objective analysis but are rooted in the cultural and aesthetic assumptions and predispositions of architects. A comparison of theoretical positions proposed by the very different figures of the English writer, Geoffrey Scott,

> The relation of construction to design is the fundamental problem of architectural aesthetics.[5]

and Le Corbusier,

> I shall no longer speak to you of poetry or lyricism. I shall draw precise reasonable things ... I shall talk 'technique' and you will react, 'poetry'.[6]

is elaborated by a comparative analysis of designs for museum buildings by Piano & Rogers and Louis Kahn, The Centre Pompidou and the Mellon Center for British Art respectively, and Robert Venturi and Carlo Scarpa, the Sainsbury Wing at the National Gallery, London, and the Castelvecchio in Verona and the Gipsoteca Canoviana at Possagno. The essay proposes, in conclusion, that questions of *technique* should be brought into the centre of the curriculum of architectural education in opposition to their all too familiar relegation to the periphery.

The two final essays turn to the subject of *sound* in relation to buildings and to the specific nature of organised sound as music. The first, 'Typology versus invention: Acoustics and the architecture of music performance', is concerned with the design of spaces for music performance – opera houses and concert halls – and is framed as an examination of the relationship between precedent, provided by preexisting cases of these building types, and the scientific theories of architectural acoustics. The study begins with Vitruvius[7] and reviews the evolution of the historical forms of each building type and the emergence of the powerful typologies, in, respectively, the seventeenth and eighteenth centuries of the 'horseshoe' auditorium for opera and the 'shoebox' hall for concert music. At the very beginning of the twentieth century, architectural acoustics was placed on a sound basis in science with the work of W.C. Sabine who, in his research at Harvard University, established the reverberation time as an objective criterion of acoustic quality.[8] The first application of his work, in the design of the New Boston Music Hall, was a confirmation of the validity of the shoebox as the dominant form for music performance. In Sabine's footsteps, the work of Bagenal and Wood in the United Kingdom and Gustave Lyon in France took the science further in the 1920s and 30s, and their work coincided with the growth of interest in the design of auditoria by the architects of the Modern Movement. The link was cemented, in 1926, with the collaboration between Lyon and Le Corbusier in the design of the assembly hall in the competition entry for the Palace of the League of Nations. Here and in many other buildings of the period, the 'fan-shape' became the preferred typology for the 'modern' concert hall. Once again, new *theory* led to a form that quickly acquired the status of precedent. The second half of the century saw a revival of the shoebox type, validated by acoustic science, in the design of the Royal Festival Hall in London, where Bagenal collaborated with the building scientists of the Building Research Station. Following this, the collaboration of Hans Scharoun and the acoustician Lothar Cremer in the conception of the 'vineyard' auditorium of the Philharmonie in Berlin opened up radical new possibilities for the design of concert halls. Into the twenty-first century, the development of new tools for computer simulation and analysis of room acoustics, the vineyard has emerged as a significant new typology with numerous successful examples, frequently conceived by major architects working with global acoustics consultants. But alongside these we have seen a notable revival of the 'shoebox' as an alternative and equally valid solution for the design of spaces for music performance. Precedent living on.

The final essay, 'Musical affinities: Aalto and Kokkonen, Scarpa and Nono', turns to a more subjective exploration of the link between architecture and music. The essay had its origin in a lecture given at the Huddersfield Contemporary Music Festival in 2003 and takes its cue from the personal friendships between two pairs of major twentieth-century artists – architects and composers, Alvar Aalto and Joonas Kokkonen in Finland and Carlo Scarpa and Luigi Nono in Italy. In the lecture, I made an audio-visual presentation in which I juxtaposed images of a building with a recording of a musical composition. These were:

Aalto: Villa Kokkonen, Jarvenpää. Kokkonen: *Cello Concerto*
Scarpa: Gipsoteca Canoviana, Possagno. Nono: *Ai Carlo Scarpa, architetto, ai suoi infiniti possibili.*

In identifying these 'affinities', I drew upon the shared cultural backgrounds of the two pairs of artists, in Finland – through the particular and individual relation of their works to the mainstream of twentieth-century European modernism – and in Italy, specifically in Venice, through the explicit dedication of Nono's composition in memory of his architect friend.

Notes

1 'Report on the Conference on Architectural Education', Magdalen College, Oxford, *Journal of the Royal Institute of British Architects*, June 1958, pp. 279–282.
2 Dean Hawkes, *The Environmental Imagination: Technics and Poetics of the Architectural Environment*, London & New York, Routledge, 1st edition 2008, 2nd edition, 2020.
3 Louis Kahn, 'Silence and Light', lecture given at ETH, Zurich, 1969, in Heinz Ronner and Shared Jhaveri, *Louis I. Kahn: Complete Works*, Basel, Birkhäuser, 1987.
4 See the following: Kenneth Frampton, 'Towards a critical regionalism: Six points for an architecture of resistance', in Hal Foster (Ed.), *Postmodern Culture*, London & Concorde, MA, Pluto Press, 1983; Victor Olgyay, *Design with Climate: Bioclimatic Approach to Architectural Regionalism*, Princeton, NJ, Princeton University Press, 1963; Alexander Tzonis and Lianne Lefaivre, *Architecture of Regionalism in a Globalised World*, London & New York, Routledge, 2012; Dean Hawkes, Jane McDonald and Koen Steemers, *The Selective Environment: An Approach to Environmentally Responsive Architecture*, London & New York, Routledge, 2002.
5 Geoffrey Scott, *The Architecture of Humanism*, London, Constable & Co., 1914.
6 Le Corbusier, *Precisions: On the Present State of Architecture and City Planning*, Paris, Cres et Cie, 1930, English translation, Cambridge, MA, MIT Press, 1991.
7 Vitruvius, *The Ten Books on Architecture*, trans. W.H. Morgan, New York, Dover Books, 1960.
8 Wallace Clement Sabine, *Collected Papers on Acoustics*, Cambridge, MA, Harvard University Press, 1922. Reprinted with Introduction by Frederick V. Hunt, New York, Dover Publications, 1964.

Essay 1[1]
The centre and the periphery
Some reflections on the nature and conduct of architectural research

Introduction

This essay, which derives from a talk given to the Martin Centre Research Society at the Department of Architecture at Cambridge in October 1994, examines the continuing relevance of the model of architectural research which was proposed at the Oxford Conference on architectural education in 1958. It suggests that the 'Oxford model', with its roots in the procedures of the sciences, in which 'fundamental' research precedes 'development' before leading into practical application, fails to account for the role of the designer in the evolution of the state of architecture. It also proposes that developments in architectural education, in particular the growth of the unit system of studio instruction, have added a further element to the productive and investigative potential of the schools of architecture and that this should be accounted for in any valid model of research.

When I joined the Cambridge School in January 1965, the head of the school, Leslie Martin, was in the process of developing a programme of research, and I worked on a project funded by the Building Research Station to investigate the relationship between daylighting standards and the form of mass housing layouts. This used scale models placed under the 'trans-illuminated domical artificial sky' that stood in the garden of the school at Scroope Terrace. This was the product of an earlier PhD project by David Croghan, who was the supervisor of the project.[2] The project was directed from the Building Research Station by R.G. Hopkinson, one of the great building scientists.[3]

1964 was just six years after the Oxford Conference on Education organised by the RIBA, which was to prove to be one of the most significant events in the development of architectural education in Britain, most particularly in the emphasis that was placed on the importance of research. By all accounts, Leslie Martin and Richard Llewelyn-Davies (who was to become head of the Bartlett School in 1960), played central roles in the debate. Martin was the author of the report of the conference, which was published in the *RIBA Journal* in June 1958.[4] There he wrote, 'Theory is the body of principles that explains and interrelates all the facts of a subject'.

DOI: 10.4324/9781003083023-2

His concern was to show that there wasn't a 'theory' of architecture to deal with the issues that confronted both education and practice at that time. He went on to say, 'Research is the tool by which theory is advanced. Without it *teaching can have no direction and thought no cutting edge*' (My italics).

In an essay with the title, 'Evolution of a Theory', published in 1992,[5] I reviewed the achievements of the 25–30 years of research in the British schools of architecture. Following the Oxford conference, schools began to establish programmes of research and to attract external funding for this. At Cambridge, Martin encouraged such developments and promoted a number of individual projects, such as David Croghan's daylighting work and the totally contrasted PhD project, submitted in the same year by Peter Eisenman on *The Formal Basis of Modern Architecture*.[6] In 1967, Martin made a great step forward when he established a centre for research that was based on three externally funded projects that, together, became the centre for Land Use and Built Form Studies.[7] A group of us got to work, more or less together, and things started to happen. At the same time, similar events occurred in other British schools and the foundations of a research culture were laid.

My review of this early research concluded that the outcome was largely positive and showed the extent and success of research as measured by a number of criteria. One such, that I regard as important in assessing the value of research in an 'applied' subject like architecture, is its value to practice. It is demonstrable that a good deal of the research that took place in schools of architecture in the 25 years or so from the mid-1960s was of benefit to practice. As an illustration, the conference held in 1992 to mark the 25th anniversary of the founding of LUBFS[8] was given the nicely ambiguous title, 'Research into Practice'. At this, a wide range of papers illustrated some of the routes by which the research had, in some way or another, influenced practice, either by being directly applied to inform a particular building project or urban design proposal, or in some more general way, by the enumeration of specific knowledge.

At the Oxford Conference, Martin and his colleagues were particularly concerned to argue that research would benefit teaching and that, consequently, this better informed teaching would benefit practice. It is difficult to demonstrate the implication that teachers who research are better teachers than those who 'just' teach, but this seems to be a reasonable proposition. Those who are actively engaged in research, in whatever aspect of architectural studies, are teaching to some extent on the basis of their own work, and it is probable that this will offer a more substantial basis from which to teach than reliance on the published works of others.

Since the 1960s, research has become a major contributor to the income of schools of architecture and is also an indicator of their standing, both within their parent institutions and in the now commonplace procedures of research assessment, such as the REF – Research Excellence Framework – that are a fact of academic life.

The problem of theory

In this review of research, I failed, however, to discover that the research that had followed from the Oxford Conference had contributed much, if anything, to one of the conference's – and Leslie Martin's – principal aims: the development of 'theory', as declared in the key statement from the report, 'Research is the tool by which theory is advanced'. By its nature and definition, the development of theory is unlikely to be a suitable subject for a research grant application.

The Concise Oxford Dictionary offers the following definition: 'supposition explaining something, especially one based on principles independent of the phenomena to be explained'. P.B. Medawar, in *The Art of the Soluble*,[9] proposed a definition of the maturity of a discipline (a theory?) as occurring when, speaking metaphorically, 'you no longer have to count the fall of every apple'. This seems to me very apt in this context. You have all-embracing principles by which you comprehend individual cases.

The dictionary goes on to offer another definition of theory as, 'speculative thought'. This is very interesting in the present discussion. Leslie Martin wrote his 'Architect's Approach to Architecture' essay, published in the *RIBA Journal* in April 1967,[10] just before the centre for Land Use and Built Form Studies was established. This was, implicitly, a manifesto for the work of the centre, in which he emphasised the significance of speculative thought by stressing, 'It is speculation that makes rational thought live; and it is rational thought that gives speculative invention its basis and its roots'. *Concise Oxford* also goes on to give us 'theory' as the 'exposition of the principles of a science'.

I have looked beyond the dictionary for other views on theory. One of my great heroes, Igor Stravinsky, when asked about the role of theory in music declared it to be, 'hindsight'.[11] Then he said, 'it doesn't exist'. Next, warming to the subject, he declared, 'There are compositions from which it is deduced, or if this is not quite true, it has a by-product existence that is powerless to create or even to justify'. He then thought more and said, 'Nevertheless, composition involves a deep intuition of theory'. This is a great man, thinking out loud, and helping to show that theory, in particular in musical composition, or I suggest by relevant analogy, in architecture, is a complex matter.

Turning to the sciences, I referred to Thomas Kuhn's, *The Structure of Scientific Revolutions*.[12] Here we find the proposition that, in science, theory must be chosen for reasons that are ultimately personal and subjective. So, wherever we seek, we find that theory is a difficult matter.

At the Oxford Conference, Martin argued that, 'without theory, research is no more than a study of techniques and parcels of this or that form of knowledge'. My analysis of the outcome of the first generation of post-Oxford research in the British schools of architecture was that this was precisely what had been achieved. There had been a large body of generally useful research across the full spectrum of the field, but this did not in sum or in part constitute a 'theory' of architecture.

An alternative model

What I want to do here is to look more widely at the nature of research in architecture, to re-evaluate the Oxford model, and to try to offer an alternative. Viewed at this distance, it appears that the model that emerged from Oxford derived from a particular and rather generalised idea of research in the scientific disciplines. The contributors to the conference were concerned to enhance the standing of the profession and saw university education as the means of achieving this – the creation of a graduate profession. At the time there were many routes into the profession, with so-called 'unrecognised' schools in a variety of institutions, art schools and technical colleges, preparing full and part-time students for the RIBA external examinations, alongside schools, often long-established, in the universities. It was against this background that universal, university-based education was attractive and that, following from this, schools of architecture would develop programmes of research on the model of other university disciplines.

In seeking to establish an approach to research in architecture, the Oxford model was, essentially, the model of the applied sciences. In this it is implied that 'pure' research leads to development, which then produces application. Research is where the fundamental thinking of a discipline takes place, which is then elaborated and transformed by a process of testing and development, which may or may not occur in the university, before emerging into the 'real world', where it informs some kind of production. In paraphrase, research is essential in order to develop useful ideas and products. In architecture, however, this model does not fit. Stravinsky's critique of the relationship between theory and practice in music – 'theory is hindsight' – is, perhaps, useful here. By paraphrase, we can suggest, 'There are *buildings* from which it is deduced', then, 'Nevertheless, *design* involves a deep intuition of theory'. Here the activity of design – practice – is brought to the centre of the discipline of architecture, which begs the question of the absence of design, its methods and its products, from the conversation of the Oxford conference and from its definition of the nature of architectural research.

It was with these thoughts in mind that I tentatively proposed an alternative model in which design, both in education and practice, is acknowledged as a mode of enquiry – as research – in architecture.[13] The most important idea offered was that architectural education should be at its heart a critique of practice. Teaching, in both the lecture room and the design studio, should be critical, and research on the broadest front, historical, theoretical and technical is, in some way, a critique of practice. But, as a teacher who combined research and practice, I proposed that the work of practitioner–teachers should have a place in the model through what I termed 'critical practice'. By this I meant that this practice would be of necessity a critical activity in which projects were subject to agendas that extended beyond the circumstances of each individual project. Collectively, a sequence of projects might constitute a process of critical inquiry analogous to a research project. In that sense, practice would become research.

One of the most significant changes in the methods of architectural education since the Oxford conference is the adoption of the unit system of studio instruction, in some instances alongside the traditional, year-based approach – in others, in place of this. I have taught in both systems and see virtues in them both. In the context of the present discussion, the unit system offers the possibility for teachers and students together speculatively to explore themes that have research content. The teaching becomes research by leading to the production of a body of work that is more than a sequence of individual projects. In some instances, teachers collect the products of their studios over a period of time and re-present them in ways by which it cumulatively becomes research by design.

If we recognise the connection between conventional research, in topics that range across the humanities and applied sciences, speculative teaching – research by design and critical practice conducted by practitioner–teachers – we begin to see a model of research that acknowledges the true nature and full range of the discipline of architecture and that exhibits the characteristics that distinguish architecture from other academic disciplines.

In order to understand the questions and the possibilities of architectural research as it has evolved in the years since the Oxford conference, we must have a model in our minds that acknowledges what schools of architecture are, and could become, to replace the less useful model proposed by the pioneers of the Oxford conference.

The architect and town planner, Lionel Brett, was president of the Royal Institute of British Architects from 1965–1967. In his presidential address, published in the *RIBA Journal*,[14] he complained about a tendency he detected in some parts of the profession to be enchanted by the attractions of disciplines other than architecture itself. A state he characterised as, 'the flight to the periphery'. In many respects, Brett's was a reactionary argument, resisting wider explorations into the nature of the discipline. But I am attracted by his insistence that whatever the value of ideas from the applied sciences and the humanities in extending the scope of architectural discourse, it is essential to maintain the place of architecture itself, the practice and production of architectural design, as the centre of the discipline.

Notes

1 This essay was first published in *Architectural Research Quarterly*, Volume 1, No. 1, Autumn, 1995, pp. 8–11.

2 David Croghan, *The Measurement of Daylight and Its Effect on the Design if Buildings and Layout Particularly in Housing Development*, PhD dissertation (unpublished), University of Cambridge, 1963.

3 R.G. Hopkinson was the author of *Architectural Physics: Lighting*, London, HMSO, 1964, which became a central theoretical reference for our work. In 1965 he moved from BRS to the Bartlett School at University College London as professor of environmental design and engineering.

4 Leslie Martin, 'Report on the Oxford Conference', *Journal of the Royal Institute of British Architects*, June 1958.

5 Dean Hawkes, 'Evolution of a Theory', *Building Design*, 3 April 1992.

6 Peter Eisenman, *The Formal Basis of Modern Architecture*, PhD dissertation, University of Cambridge, 1963. Facsimile edition published, with an afterword by Peter Eisenman, Baden, Lars Müller, 2006.

7 See Essay 4, 'Bridging the cultures: Architecture, models and computers in 1960s Cambridge' for a detailed description of the work of the three 'founding' projects at LUBFS.

8 In 1974, following Leslie Martin's retirement from the Cambridge school, LUBFS was renamed in his honour as the Martin Centre for Architectural and Urban Studies.

9 P.B. Medawar, *The Art of the Soluble*, London, Methuen, 1967.

10 Leslie Martin, 'Architect's Approach to Architecture', *Journal of the Royal Institute of British Architects*, April 1967.

11 Robert Craft, *Conversations with Igor Stravinsky*, London, Faber and Faber Ltd., 1959.

12 Thomas Kuhn, *The Structure of Scientific Revolutions*, Chicago, IL & London, The University of Chicago Press, 1970.

13 These ideas were first presented at a meeting held at the Institute for Advanced Architectural Studies at the University of York, in 1994, to discuss the place of research and design in both practice and education.

14 Lionel Brett (1913–2004), President of the Royal Institute of British Architects, 1965–67.

Essay 2[1]
The architect and the academy

Introduction

In Essay 1, I argued that the adoption of a model, or perhaps, models, borrowed from the procedures of, respectively, the humanities and the sciences does not constitute a sufficient basis from which to define the nature and content of the discipline of architecture. The present essay returns to this theme and develops further the proposition that design practice, both in its processes and products, constitutes the core, the centre, of the discipline and goes on to examine the implications of this for the form, content and delivery of architectural education.

In a wide-ranging essay Robert Maxwell illustrated the history of the relationship between architectural education and practice.[2] In this he revealed the complexities, contradictions and tensions which have occurred, and continue to occur, as the two realms have evolved. In the present essay, I try to examine the question of education and practice from a different but, I think, complementary perspective. My concern hinges around the question of how we may define the term 'the discipline of architecture', and what that definition implies for schools of architecture.

My dictionaries offer the following:

> 'Dis'cipline (n) Branch of instruction: system of rules for conduct',[3] and 'A system of rules or method of practise. The studies collectively embraced in a course of learning'.[4]

The definitions make clear the connection and, perhaps, the distinction between 'instruction' and 'learning', on the one hand, and 'conduct' and 'practice' on the other and, in addition, imply the necessary connection between these – that education and practice are mutually dependent. I want now to explore the nature of this link, first as a general proposition and, then, as it applies specifically to architecture.

In 'The centre and the periphery', I refer to Igor Stravinsky's discourse on the relationship between theory and practice in musical composition.[5] In this he made the significant and characteristically cryptic observation

DOI: 10.4324/9781003083023-3

that theory is 'hindsight', that, 'There are compositions from which it is deduced.' In other words, he is pointing out that in music and, I would argue by analogy, in architecture, the elucidation of theory, or as Robert Maxwell proposes, of *Theories*, depends upon the preexistence of a body of products, works of music or architecture, that are the outcome of the activity of composers or of architects, therefore of *practice*. The implication of this for the definition of the discipline of architecture is that its foundations will reside in the production of practice.

To draw a further analogy with a 'cognate discipline', is that the academic study of architecture is based on the 'literature' of architecture, that is the buildings, in the same way that the teaching of English in the university rests upon its critical engagement with the canon of written literature, the plays, the poems, the novels. In a review of the English Faculty at Cambridge, Stephen Heath[6] tells how the study of English acquired its independence from its lowly status as 'an optional language in the Modern and Mediaeval Tripos', in the years following the First World War. This development represented the victory of the 'literary and critical' over the 'philological and linguistic'. The curriculum, as it was first taught in 1926, embraced, 'English literature, life and thought from Chaucer on', in its first part and more comparative and specialised periods in the second. The study of these works was informed by courses in critical theory and method, which soon came to be dominated by the approaches of I.A. Richards and F.R. Leavis. The translation of this model to apply to architecture is, seemingly, straightforward. We teach students about the buildings and how to analyse and interpret their nature and meaning.

There are, of course, many differences between the academic study of architecture and English, and of the most importance may be the significance of the practitioner. Robert Maxwell's essay[7] shows how, even allowing for their very different histories, architectural education in France and Britain grew out of the evolving needs of practice. This meant that the distinction between practitioner and scholar, artist and critic, which existed at the foundation of the academic English department and was central to its very conception, was less clear-cut in architecture. Until the relatively recent emergence of university courses in 'Creative Writing', the teaching of English in British universities has been exclusively in the hands of scholars and practitioners remained on the outside. In architecture, on the other hand, the converse applied. The idea that a teacher could, or should, teach without a base in practice is a relatively recent development and, in many respects, springs from the attempt to 'academicise' the discipline.

The Oxford legacy

The aim of the Royal Institute of British Architects' Conference on Architectural Education, held in Oxford in 1958, was to redefine and clarify the nature and methods of architectural education as it was then practised in Britain. Because of the essentially pragmatic way in which the schools had evolved in Britain, there was little or no academic tradition. Many of the schools were in institutions, such as art schools, that had few resources for teaching the growing technical content of design practice and, at the time, did not award degrees to their graduates; there was very little, if any, research. The conference concluded that architects should, in future, be educated in university level institutions to guarantee the creation of a graduate profession. This raised the possibility that architecture might, indeed should, justify its status within the university by acquiring the characteristics of an academic discipline. The key to this would be the creation of a coherent body of research.

In my analysis in Essay 1, I outlined how this was addressed by borrowing established models of research from the humanities and the applied sciences. In a memorable statement in his report on the conference, Leslie Martin declared, 'Theory is the body of principles that explains and interrelates all the facts of a subject. Research is the tool by which theory advances. Without it, teaching can have no direction and thought, no cutting edge'.[8] This could equally refer to the founding of the Cambridge English Faculty, where the 'facts' are the texts to be studied through the mechanism of critical theory. Alongside this analogy with the humanities, the Oxford prescription also implicitly referred to the model of applied science. In this, research has a quite explicit relationship to practice, or more generally, to industry, in proceeding through a sequence in which research discovers new knowledge, which then is taken through a phase of development before, finally, reaching application in industry.

In the last 30 years or so, research in many schools of architecture has grown and flourished under the Oxford model. Much of the work has borne fruit in numerous publications, conference and journal papers, not least in the establishment of properly refereed architectural journals[9] and in growing numbers of scholarly books. There are also instances where research has indirectly or directly informed practice. It has also, in many ways, informed teaching. In other words, architecture appears to merit its claims to the status of a *discipline*. It now stands respectably within the university. In the particular, some would say *peculiar*, circumstances of university funding in Britain, those schools of architecture that have successfully followed this path now benefit by receiving a substantial proportion of their income as a direct result of peer assessment of the quantity and quality of their research output.

All of this seems to be a success story. Why then do I, as one of the generation of architectural academics who have benefitted enormously from the Oxford legacy, feel that this paradigm has run its course? In Essay 1 I argued that, in spite of this success, Leslie Martin's conviction that research would be the essential tool for the advancement of theory has not been fulfilled. This is not to say that the field of theory in architecture has not advanced in the past 30 years. I think, however, that it can be argued that the developments that have occurred have not benefitted significantly from this formal academicisation of the discipline. But this is not the principal source of my unease. That lies in the way in which the emphasis on 'scholarship' in the history and theory of architecture and in architectural science[10] has diminished the role and status of the academic practitioner. This is not a universal problem. There are many countries in which distinguished practitioners hold senior positions in education, but it is increasingly the case in Britain, and the model has growing support elsewhere. I want to argue that this compromises the quality of architectural education, both intellectually and practically and, ultimately, will diminish the standing of the discipline, both in and out of the academy.

The architect *in* the academy – theory, practice and education

To explore this proposition I will, first, return to my analogy with cognate disciplines. Stravinsky's view of the status of theory in music was made from the perspective of a practitioner. In the present discussion, its significance lies in his acute awareness that the primary source of innovation in music derives from the activity of composers and practitioners, and theoreticians and academics contribute to the development of the art – or discipline – through the elucidation of critical commentaries upon the established and – a crucial point – ever-growing body of musical 'literature' that is created by the act of composition. This is not to deny the significance and value of critical theory in influencing the development of a discipline, in giving substance to teaching and, hence, in some way informing practice. The evidence for this is clear in many fields, most so perhaps in the study of English, where critical theory has built upon and advanced far from the methods and achievements of Richards and Leavis. I am convinced that effective practice in any field must be founded on a coherently held theoretical position, but I am equally certain that theory only goes so far in informing practice. All worthwhile practice demands some degree of invention in which theory is questioned, extended, perhaps distorted in the quest for an appropriate solution to the specific circumstances of the project. Again, Igor Stravinsky helps to illustrate the point. In his *Charles Eliot Norton Lectures*, delivered at Harvard University in 1939,[11] Stravinsky spoke about harmony in music,

> Harmony as it is taught today in the schools dictates rules that were not fixed until long after the publication of the works upon which they were based, rules which were unknown to the composers of these works. In this manner our harmonic treatises take as their point of departure Mozart and Haydn, neither of whom ever heard of harmonic treatises.

One of the principal functions of the schools of architecture – the academies – is to educate future practitioners. (Note that here I have deliberately chosen 'educate' in preference to 'train'. This is a distinction that I believe must be precisely drawn and carefully maintained.) The physical and pedagogical heart of all schools of architecture is the design studio, and it is this that most clearly differentiates architectural education and the academic discipline of architecture from most other fields. It is in the studio that the lessons of scholarship, in history, theory and architectural science are, or should be, brought to bear on the conception and development of designs. In the best schools this undoubtedly takes place, but the question arises about the way in which academic knowledge should be interpreted to sustain the act of invention that lies at the heart of designing.

It is here that practising designers can and must make a central contribution. It is, of course, possible to teach design successfully from a theoretical rather than a practical platform – there is overwhelming evidence in many schools that this is true – but I contend that the academic practitioner brings unique insights to bear on the process of interpretation and invention. At this central point in my argument, I will review a selection of statements concerning teaching made by, or in one case, made about, eminent academic practitioners.

Hertzberger and Kahn

Hermann Hertzberger directly addressed the question in his book, *Lessons for Students in Architecture*.[12] He wrote,

> It is inevitable that the work that you do as an architect should serve as a point of departure for your teaching, and obviously the best way to explain what you have to say is to do so on the basis of practical experience: that, indeed, is the common thread of this book ... When you discuss your own work, you have to ask what you acquired from whom. Because everything you find comes from somewhere. The source was not your own mind, but was supplied by the culture you belong to ... The examples and influences which abound in this book constitute the cultural context within which an architect works, and an impression is given of the range of concepts and mental images that must serve as his tools ... The capacity to find a fundamentally different solution to a problem ... depends entirely on the wealth of your experience, just as a person's expressive potential in terms of language cannot transcend that which is expressible with his vocabulary ... The aim of my 'lessons' has always been to stimulate students, to evoke in them an architectural frame of mind that will enable them to do their own work.

Louis Kahn was one of the greatest architect–teachers of modern times. Speaking in 1960, at a meeting of the Association of Collegiate Schools of Architecture, he began,

> As you know, I am a teacher which means really that I am teaching myself, and whatever rubs off, the student gets. When questions are

brought before you by students, I feel that the answers to those questions cannot be given off hand. I have always felt rather humble in the presence of a student.

During the time when I was thinking about form and design and making distinctions between the two, I thought that the unmeasureable aspects of our existence are the ones that are the most important. Such things as thought, feeling, realization are all unmeasureable. It seems that this is also the concern of scientists.

I am concerned with realization because I believe that from realization we really do design. Realization stems from the transcendence of our own feeling into the feeling of ourselves as others, and it actually represents the fact of feeling itself. The transcendence of thought is philosophy. We live by our own feelings and our own thoughts but when we come to realizations we transcend our own feelings and our own thoughts. Realization, I feel, stems from the fact of thought and the fact of feeling.

Now I say all of this because I believe one can understand a form much better when one understands realization. You might say that realization is the sense of harmony of systems and belongs to that which wants to exist and is a sense of the order of things.

Design, when we come to it, is that which we call on to put into being that which we realize.[13]

Scarpa and Zumthor

Throughout most of his working life, Carlo Scarpa combined practice and teaching in Venice. My example of his pedagogy is a description, by a former pupil, of a Scarpa lesson.

My encounter with Carlo Scarpa goes back to my student days. Mine was the generational privilege of hearing him speak *ex cathedra*, or even more of seeing him, for his expressiveness went far beyond words alone. As a lecturer he made a deep impression on me, and I shall never forget his account of how he solved the problem of displaying the *Syracuse Annunciation* at the exhibition of paintings by Antonello da Messina. Scarpa explained that this painting was so fragmented that the surviving pieces tended to be viewed separately from one another. Harsh lighting would have produced an undesirable clinical effect, making viewing like an autopsy. The light filtering through the window in the exhibition hall was a pitiless white, showing up the shreds of that glorious painting and making it harder to respond to the cold tones of the landscape and the severe construction of the interior. Waving his hand about as if to make us feel the impalpable lightness of a drapery, the lecturer described how he had gone out to a haberdasher's and bought a nylon underskirt, very lightly tinted. This he set, at a suitable distance between the exterior light and the window drapery, so that the light was mellowed without being dimmed.

Without wishing to overemphasise the relevance of this lesson, I should like to note one or two things about it. First, the starting point was Scarpa's intuition of the specific qualities of that work of art. Second, his perception of light was not just in terms of direction and intensity but also colour.[14]

The connection between practice and teaching is strongly demonstrated in the work of Peter Zumthor. Just when his refined and subtle architecture achieved international recognition, he joined the faculty of the newly opened Accademia do Architettura at Mendrisio in Switzerland. Writing on 'Teaching architecture, learning architecture', Zumthor has stated,

> Young people go to university with the aim of becoming architects, of finding out if they have what it takes. What is the first thing we should teach them?
>
> First of all, we must explain to them that the person standing in front of them is not someone who asks questions whose answers he already knows. Practising architecture is about asking oneself questions, finding one's own answers with the help of the teacher, whittling down, finding solutions. Over and over again.
>
> The strength of a good design lies in ourselves and in our ability to perceive the world with both emotion and reason. A good architectural design is sensuous. A good architectural design is intelligent.
>
> We all experience architecture before we have even heard the word. The roots of architectural understanding lie in our architectural experience: our room, our house, our street, our village, our town, our landscape – we experience them all early on, unconsciously, and we subsequently compare them with the countryside, towns and houses we experience later on. The roots of our understanding of architecture lie in our biography. Students have to learn to work consciously with their personal biographical experiences of architecture.[15]

Each of these statements shows how the architect's teaching is profoundly influenced by his practice. Hermann Hertzberger is quite explicit in speaking of the way in which his work is influenced by his extensive knowledge of 'references' to the works of other architects, to vernacular buildings, to images drawn from painting, all of which are illustrated in his book. These references are the 'literature' of architecture and what he does in his practice is to draw upon and interpret this. From this process comes, 'The capacity to find a fundamentally different solution to the problem.' Louis Kahn makes no reference to specific sources. For him, teaching is a process of self-discovery and, 'whatever rubs off, the student gets'. He is concerned with the primacy of the unmeasureable, of 'thought, feeling, realization'. His lessons constantly stressed the need to penetrate beneath the pragmatic facts of the building programme and to discover, through the act of realisation, 'the sense of harmony of systems … that which wants to exist'. Peter Zumthor also believes that teaching is a process of discovery, that in architecture the answers are not already known. His position shares some ground with Herman Hertzberger in his insistence on the necessity of 'experience' as a condition of 'understanding', but his definition of experience includes a student's 'personal biographical experiences of architecture', in addition to academic knowledge. Finally, Carlo Bertelli's description of Scarpa's lesson reveals the way in which an account of a specific event in his practice was used to demonstrate universal principles about light in architectural space.

I suggest that insights such as these and the ability to communicate them through the medium of teaching depend on these architects' deep experience of practice. Practice, when it is conducted at the level achieved by them, becomes a kind of 'laboratory' in which method is tested and validated through the acts of designing and building. It is from this 'proof' that their teaching acquires its particular authority.

Substance or assessment

The central point in the controversy in the debate about the status of design practice in the academic system is whether design can be considered to be research. David Yeomans reviewed this problem in the specific context of the bureaucratic and pragmatic arrangements that then were applied to the process of research assessment in British universities.[16] In this he stated that 'The argument that design is research simply will not stand up'. This is because, he claimed, architectural design does not match the criteria which apply to the definition of research as it is understood in a university department of engineering. Engineering research, he suggested, is concerned with 'general issues, classes of problems and … general solutions', and architectural design fails to meet any of these criteria. Yeomans also rejects the proposition that architectural design is analogous to output in music or the fine arts, on the grounds that these fields do not have to meet the same demands of clients and site conditions which apply to architecture. 'An analogy with painting or music reduces architecture to *mere* (my italics) architectural composition' – as if there is no justification for any knowledge base other than a body of precedents or aesthetic models.

The problem with these arguments is that, with their preoccupation with the process of research assessment, they fail to address the more fundamental question of what we define by the academic discipline of architecture. The question should not be, 'Can design be research?' but 'What constitutes the substance of the discipline of architecture and how should *this* be assessed?' In Essay 1, 'The centre and the periphery', I proposed that, 'Whatever we do in a school of architecture is a *critical* activity. It is the function of the academic in architecture to conduct a continuing critique of the state of practice'. This critical function is, or should be, central to scholarship and research in both the architectural humanities and in architectural science. But this should also include the work of teachers who practise, who, therefore, carry out 'critical practice'.

The work of the four architect–teachers who are discussed previously is clearly *critical* in precisely this sense. The quality of their designs implicitly represents a critical commentary on the production of ordinary practice. But, more significantly, their work adds to the built 'literature' of the discipline through its widespread diffusion by the international network of architectural publication. There, it is subject to critical commentary and, thereby, constitutes essential material for the academic discourse, just as new novels, poems and plays add to the material of the academic discipline of English and compositions to that of Music. In many instances, architect–teachers also contribute directly to the critical discourse by writing descriptively and critically about their built works and, often with profound insight, about the works of others.

It seems folly to exclude practising architects from the academy purely because they and their work do not conform to the demands of a bureaucratic process of assessment. It is, of course, essential that their practice should meet criteria that distinguish it from what may be termed 'ordinary' practice, but there is a growing body of evidence to show that this distinction may be quite easily drawn. To define what is understood when we speak of 'research' we should examine the nature and procedures of the discipline and not, arbitrarily, apply models derived from other fields. Architecture may fit uneasily within the limits of the models of the humanities or the applied sciences, but this suggests that we should seek to define a model which acknowledges its unique characteristics as a discipline. This, of necessity, embraces aspects of the humanities and the sciences, but the core of the discipline lies in the centrality of design, of critical practice and in the products of that practice. Perhaps I may, in conclusion, rephrase Leslie Martin's Oxford conference declaration:

> Theory is the body of principles which explains and interrelates all the facts of a *discipline*. Research and *critical practice* are the tools by which theory is advanced. Without these, teaching can have no direction and thought, no cutting edge.

Notes

1 This essay was first published in *Architectural Research Quarterly*, Volume 4, No. 1, 2000, pp. 35–39.
2 Robert Maxwell, 'Education for the creative act', *Architectural Research Quarterly*, Volume 4, No. 1, 2000, pp. 55–65.
3 Discipline, *Concise Oxford Dictionary*, Oxford, Oxford University Press, 1964.

4 Discipline, *The Practical Standard Dictionary*, New York & London, Funk and Wagnalls, 1928.

5 Robert Craft, *Conversations with Igor Stravinsky*, London, Faber & Faber, 1959.

6 Stephen Heath, 'I.A. Richards, F.R. Leavis and Cambridge English', in Richard Mason (Ed.), *Cambridge Minds*, Cambridge, Cambridge University Press, 1994.

7 Robert Maxwell, op cit.

8 Leslie Martin, 'Report on the Oxford Conference', *RIBS Journal*, June 1958.

9 In Britain, *Architectural Research Quarterly* and *The Journal of Architecture* were both founded in 1995.

10 The term 'architectural science' has, with some reason, gained currency in recent years. It may be defined as the applied science, of materials, construction, structures and environment that is taught in schools of architecture and, and such, is useful. It does *not*, however, constitute a *science* of architecture. That remains one of the unfulfilled projects of the discipline. In his book, *Architecture*, published in 1911, W.R. Lethaby hinted at the possibility of such a science when he wrote, 'Some day we shall get a morphology of the art by some architectural Linneaus or Darwin'. *That* may have been architectural science. On these grounds, in my own work I prefer, pedantically, to refer to *building* science.

11 Igor Stravinsky, Charles Eliot Norton Lectures, published as, *Poetics of Music: In the Form of Six Lessons*, Cambridge, MA, Harvard University Press, 1942.

12 Hermann Hertzberger, *Lessons for Students in Architecture*, Rotterdam, Uitgeverij 010 Publishers, 1991.

13 Louis I. Kahn, 'On form and design', speech at 46th meeting of the Association of Collegiate Schools of Architecture held at the University of Berkeley, Berkeley, CA, 22–23 April 1960. In Alexandra Latour (Ed.), *Louis I. Kahn: Writings, Lectures, Interviews*, New York, Rizzoli International, 1991.

14 Carlo Bertelli, 'Light and design', in Francesco Dal Co and Giuseppe Mazzariol (Eds.), *Carlo Scarpa: The Complete Works*, English Edition, London, The Architectural Press, 1986.

15 Peter Zumthor, 'Teaching architecture, learning architecture', in *Thinking Architecture*, Basel, Boston, MA, & Berlin, Birkhäuser – Publishers for Architecture, 1996.

16 David Yeomans, 'Can design be called research?', *Architectural Research Quarterly*, Volume 1, No. 1, 1995, pp. 12–15.

Essay 3[1]
The shaping of architectural research

Transatlantic transactions

Introduction

The growth of formalised research has been one of the most important developments in architectural education in the last half-century. It is now axiomatic that most, if not all, faculty members in schools of architecture will undertake some measure of research. In this the academic architect stands alongside, and is indistinguishable from, colleagues in other disciplines. But in the middle decades of the last century the case for the development of research culture in architecture was not so clear-cut. Two of the central figures in the debate were Serge Chermayeff (Figure 3.1) in the United States and Leslie Martin (Figure 3.2) in the United Kingdom.

One of the first points to establish is the trail of connections between the lives and works of Chermayeff and Martin. They were almost exact contemporaries, Chermayeff, 1900–1996, Martin, 1908–2000. In the 1930s they moved in overlapping circles. In 1934 Martin became head of the School of Architecture at Hull and Chermayeff was one of the first of an impressive array of visiting lecturers he invited. Others included Marcel Breuer, Walter Gropius and Erich Mendelsohn. Their mutual friendships with artists Ben Nicholson and Naum Gabo led to the inclusion of designs by Chermayeff in *Circle*, the 'International Survey of Constructive Art' that Martin, Nicholson and Gabo edited in 1937.[2]

If we compare their respective academic careers, the significant period for the present discussion spans from the middle of the 1950s to early in the 1970s. Chermayeff held professorships at Harvard, 1953–1962, and Yale, 1962–1969. Martin was professor and head of department at Cambridge, 1956–1972. Chermayeff's arrival at Harvard followed important appointments at Brooklyn College, New York and the Chicago Design Institute. Martin went to Cambridge from the London County Council, where he was Deputy Architect, 1948–1953, and Architect, 1953–1956.

A number of individuals established important connections between the 'two Cambridges'. First is that forged by Christopher Alexander. He read Mathematics and Architecture at the English Cambridge, just when Martin

DOI: 10.4324/9781003083023-4

Figure 3.1 Serge Chermayeff, portrait. (RIBA Collections)

became head of the school. He crossed the Atlantic in 1959 to begin his PhD studies at the Joint Center for Urban Studies, Harvard and MIT (Cambridge, MA), under Chermayeff's supervision. This influential work was published in 1967 as *Notes on the Synthesis of Form*.[3]

A second key figure is Lionel March. He also read Mathematics and Architecture in the British Cambridge and followed Alexander to the Joint Center for Urban Studies. Shortly after his arrival, Alexander left for Berkeley, and March has recorded that this left him and Kevin Lynch as the only architects in the Centre, 'dominated by lawyers, economists and political scientists'. His studies there were abandoned when Leslie Martin invited him to return to Britain to work on the 'Whitehall Plan'.[4] In 1967, March became the assistant director of the newly founded centre for Land Use and Built Form Studies (LUBFS) in the Cambridge school and, soon afterwards, its director. Subsequently, he returned to the United States where he became professor of architecture and computation at the University of California, Los Angeles.[5]

The third link in the chain is John Meunier. He was a graduate of the Liverpool School of Architecture and, as a student at the Graduate School of Design at Harvard, was one of Chermayeff and Alexander's collaborators in the research for and publication of *Community and Privacy*.[6] He then became

Figure 3.2 Leslie Martin, portrait. (Architectural Press Archive/RIBA Collections)

an influential member of Martin's teaching staff at Cambridge. At this time, he practised in parallel with his teaching and was responsible for a number of notable buildings, most significantly the Burrell Museum in Glasgow, designed with colleagues in the school, Barry Gasson and Brit Andressen. In 1976, he moved back to the United States to take up senior teaching posts, first at Cincinnati and then at Arizona State University in Phoenix.

The foundations of architectural research

In the mid-1950s, in both the United States and Britain, there was widespread debate about the aims and methods of architectural education. Chermayeff and Martin both played leading roles in this.

In 1950, in a paper on 'Architecture at the Chicago Institute of Design',[7] Chermayeff declared that, 'the revaluation of educational responsibility in the field of architecture becomes crucial and the fundamental revisions in the total structure of professional training essential'. He stated the immediate objectives as:

- The restatement of principles: The uninhibited measuring of every phase of existing practice against the yardstick of scientific knowledge, technical efficiency and plastic sensibility of the highest order of which we are capable.

- The establishment in the student's mind that architectural activity carries with it social responsibility and the ethics of comprehensively grasped new order beyond the lesser requirements of technical and business efficiency.

Later, and after the experience of his time at Harvard, Chermayeff made a more general statement in a paper to a seminar of the AIA – ACSA (American Institute of Architects – Association of Collegiate Schools of Architecture).[8]

> [S]chools are by definition scholarly, exploratory, intellectually adventurous, philosophical; that is what I mean by theory and principles is that they are philosophically long-term minded. Their interest is to deepen and widen the field as a whole without exaggerated regard for the immediately familiar and practical. Their method is imaginative inquiry. This is true in relation to architecture in the larger sense of the word, in schools which have planning and other related departments and, of course, more particularly in universities with great extra-departmental facilities and resources. The search for widening and deepening is not only a moral but an intellectual obligation, and the student and the teacher and the researcher, in spite of themselves ... have become in fact opponents of the practitioner.

Leslie Martin's first major public statement on the question of architectural education was his report on the RIBA Conference on Architectural Education that was held at Magdalen College, Oxford in April 1958.[9] Before this the last formal debate on architectural education in Britain had taken place in 1924. Martin, with the support of like-minded colleagues, such as Richard Llewellyn-Davies – who was to become head of the Bartlett School at University College London in 1960 – established a clear agenda for the conference.

- The needs of the profession and the community and the desirable standards
- The means of education, the routes of entry into the profession and the standards that are being, and could be, achieved
- Developments of advanced training and research

Underlying the agenda was the question of the status of architectural education in general and its place within the universities. At the time, only half of the students attended the so-called 'recognised' schools of architecture, usually those in universities. Others followed full and part-time routes at a wide variety of institutions. The argument of the Oxford conference was that all students should attend university level institutions and that architecture should legitimise its place in the university through the development of *theory* and that the basis of theory is *research*. In a key paragraph of his report, Martin wrote,

> If architecture is to take its proper place in the university and if the knowledge which it entails is to be taught at the highest standard, it will be necessary to establish a bridge between faculties, between the arts and the sciences, engineering science, sociology and economics. Furthermore the universities will require something more than a study of techniques and parcels of this or that kind of knowledge. They will expect and have a right to expect that knowledge will be guided and developed by principles: that is, by theory. 'Theory' is the body of principles that explains and interrelates all the facts of a subject. Research is the tool by which theory is advanced. Without it, teaching can have no direction and thought, no cutting edge.

The language and circumstances of the respective statements are different: Chermayeff, passionate and personal; Martin, measured and formal. But they articulate similar concerns, and both argue that *research* is central to the redefinition of the discipline of architecture in addressing the new needs of society, in transforming the basis of architectural education and, hence, of practice.

Almost immediately upon his arrival at Harvard in 1953, Chermayeff began to mount the argument for the establishment of research study. In a memorandum to the Dean, Josep-Lluis Sert, dated 5 November 1953, Chermayeff wrote

> Generally speaking, it appears of the utmost importance to inaugurate this activity (Doctorate Study) in the Graduate School of Design, so that it might be in fact what at the moment it is only in name. With this in view, I would recommend most strongly that all possible effort be invested in obtaining funds for the establishment of fellowships in the philosophic, artistic and practical aspects of the total design field.[10]

In April 1955, Chermayeff made a proposal to a Faculty Meeting of the Graduate School of Design.[11]

> That the Faculty of Design recommend to the Governing Board the authorization of a program for advanced studies in the Graduate School of Design, as follows:
>
> I. PROGRAM
>
> That in addition to the curricula leading to professional degrees in Architecture, Landscape Architecture and City Planning, the Graduate School of Design undertake advanced studies of problems of Design in these three fields.

The program is not intended to furnish further training for professional practice but is intended to provide opportunities for those who plan to do advanced research or want to enter the teaching fields.

Emphasis will be on research through design action in such a manner as to encourage and to facilitate concerted work around problems which will bring together to bear upon a single task, humanists, artists, scientists and technicians.

Following his move from Harvard to Yale in 1962, Chermayeff continued to pursue and elaborate this line of inquiry. In 1964, he made a proposal for the introduction of an Advanced Studies Fellowship Program at the Yale School of Architecture.[12] This was intended to,

round out and fill gaps by investigating various aspects of architectural designs. The work would be undertaken by mature, experienced and talented students.

The intention is to develop long term ideas and principles ... and not to seek direct technical solutions to any particular problem.

In 1966 Chermayeff was successful in obtaining funds from the US Bureau of Standards to support a project in 'Advanced Studies in Urban Environment'. The aim was, 'To make the Master Class at Yale under Professor Chermayeff a nucleus for interdepartmental studies in urban organization and design'. The project, on which Alexander Tzonis played a major role as a Fellow, was based on a series of seminars at which a sequence of contemporary urban design types from around the world were subjected to critical evaluation by Faculty and visitors.

Across the Atlantic, Leslie Martin, as head of the department at Cambridge, did not have to adopt such formal procedures to introduce a new level and mode of research activity. The university had well-established general regulations for the conduct and awarding of research degrees, which could be adopted in architecture. In the early years, these provided the framework for the initiation of a number of individual PhD projects.[13]

In 1966, Martin and Lionel March published as short, but crucial, essay, 'Land Use and Built Forms', in the journal, *Cambridge Research*.[14] This articulated for the first time the geometrical principles underlying the initial stage of the body of work that was about to begin. The major step forward came in 1967, with the establishment of the centre for Land Use and Built Form Studies (LUBFS – later renamed in his honour as the Martin Centre for Architectural and Urban Studies). This came about when Martin was successful in obtaining major research grants to support projects at three distinct architectural scales. These were the *Offices Study*, funded by the Ministry of Public Buildings and Works; the *Universities Study*, funded by the Nuffield Foundation; and the *Urban Systems Study*, funded by the

Centre for Environmental Studies. These projects supported six full-time research assistants, all of whom were architecture graduates.[15]

The shape of architectural research

Whilst it is clear that there was much common ground, both ideologically and methodologically, in the work that came out of the two Cambridges, it is their differences that were almost certainly of greater significance. A brief list of the principal publications from each 'school' serves to illustrate this and begin some kind of discussion (Table 3.1).

The similarities and differences between the two may be summarised by comparing *Community and Privacy* with *Urban Space and Structures*. Chermayeff and Alexander offer a passionate polemic about, 'The conflicts between private freedom and public responsibility'. The book begins by declaring that,

> The human population of the world and its productive capacity are reaching dimensions that defy the individual imagination. Today billions of people are demanding accommodations of all kinds, moving at ever greater speeds, communicating over vast distances in no time at all, and urbanizing at astonishing densities ... Man has not yet developed a strategy for organizing huge quantities although he has perfected techniques for computing them.
>
> In this book, some problems in making the human habitat and in shaping man's physical environment are tackled head-on in the belief that if the special contemporary characteristics of the physical

Table 3.1 Research publications

Chermayeff	*Martin*
S. Chermayeff and C. Alexander, *Community and Privacy*, Doubleday & Co., New York, 1963.	L. Martin and L. March (eds.), *Urban Space and Structures*, Cambridge University Press, Cambridge, UK, 1972.
S. Chermayeff and A. Tzonis, *The Shape of Community*, Penguin Books, London and Baltimore, 1971.	L. Martin, *Buildings and Ideas: 1933-1983*, Cambridge University Press, Cambridge, UK, 1983.
S. Chermayeff, (Richard Pluntz, ed.), *Design and the Public Good*, MIT Press, Cambridge, MA & London, 1981.	L. March (ed.), *The Architecture of Form*. Cambridge University Press, Cambridge, UK, 1976.
C. Alexander, *Notes on the Synthesis of Form*, Harvard University Press, Cambridge, MA, 1964.	P. Carolin & T. Dannatt, *Architecture, Education and Research: The Work of Leslie Martin: Papers and Selected Articles*, Academy Editions, London, 1996.

environment are recognized at the eleventh hour, the task of designing can be advanced in a forthright way and further erosion of the human habitat can be prevented.

In their Foreword to *Urban Space and Structures*, Martin and March wrote, with characteristic restraint, that,

> More and more the environment of the world is manmade; in its own right it deserves serious study. The papers … in this … volume describe and illustrate the growth of a particular attitude of thought that has been building up around architectural studies in Cambridge in the last few years … these studies tend to remove the distinctions between architecture and planning, between design of individual buildings and the collective choice of the shape of the environment.[16]

Chermayeff and Alexander were out to change the world. Martin and March were to subject it to 'serious study'. But, behind these differences of style, the issues are compellingly similar.

This distinction is, unsurprisingly, carried through into the nature of the work itself. Out of the critique of *Community and Privacy* emerges two powerful strands of argument – one abstract, the other specifically concrete. The abstraction is in Alexander's contribution, derived from his work on the Synthesis of Form, that juxtaposes 'Faith and Reason' and develops, using computerised matrix analysis, a systematic approach to the statement of the problem of design. The logic of this is then transferred to the promotion of the virtues of the court house form as a specific solution to the problem of urban housing.

The key to Martin and March's approach is also mathematical, and computer methods played their part in much of the work. But the fundamental mathematical idea is a simple, if powerful, geometrical abstraction, the Fresnel square, which serves to sustain a strikingly simple observation about alternative, *generic*, approaches to built form – a comparison of the court and pavilion. Out of this came a series of studies, both abstract and concrete, and at scales from the regional to the individual building, that constituted a significant critique of the conventional wisdom of practice. In a paper delivered at the RIBA in London in 1967,[17] Martin stated that,

> The ultimate problem for the profession is that of setting out the possibilities and choices in building an environment. And in that field the crisis will not be solved by technical advance alone, or by picturesque images. At bottom it is a crisis of lack of understanding. Our task is to try to make that understanding more complete.

Research and practice

Serge Chermayeff and Leslie Martin were both distinguished practitioners. Their careers in practice followed quite different paths, but, I suggest, their experience of practice was important in shaping their approach to research when they entered architectural education.

Following his arrival in America, Chermayeff's built work consisted almost entirely of private houses, most notably that he built for himself in 1963 at 29 Lincoln Street in New Haven. As Alan Powers has pointed out,[18] these buildings may be interpreted as an integral part of the themes that became formalised and elaborated in the research programmes that he developed at Harvard and Yale. Indeed, it may be suggested that the preoccupation with the social zoning of the dwelling that became central to the research was already in evidence in Bentley Wood, the house, also for himself, that he built in England in 1938, before his departure for the United States (Figure 3.3).

Leslie Martin arrived at Cambridge with the experience of his years at the LCC Architect's Department behind him. In Cambridge, his practice flourished and, with a succession of distinguished associates, he was responsible for a sequence of internationally acknowledged buildings.[19] These included major projects for the universities at Oxford and Cambridge. The Manor Road Library (1959) (Figure 3.4) and the Zoology and Psychology building, both at Oxford, benefitted from the use of the artificial sky at the Cambridge school[20] in the development of their form and detail as an early demonstration of the link between research in the school and practice.

Figure 3.3 Serge Chermayeff, House at Bentley Wood, East Sussex. (Architectural Press Archive/RIBA Collections)

Figure 3.4 Leslie Martin, Manor Road Libraries, Oxford. (John Donat/RIBA Collections)

Chermayeff's and Martin's continuing engagement in practice in parallel with their academic activities, different though it was, invested their work with particular qualities. The agenda of research was inevitably shaped, to some degree, by perceptions gained from practice and practice was given substance by the clarity of purpose that flowed from the methods of research.

A basis for education and practice

In drawing together the strands of this inquiry, I am struck by the conviction that Chermayeff and Martin so demonstrably shared, to establish a basis for both architectural education and practice, that was founded on objective analysis of fundamental programmatic questions and on the use of rational procedures for the production of designs. They both saw this as a necessary resistance to the dangers of subjectivity and stylism. By the 1960s, the first rumblings of post-modernism represented a threat to the realisation of the rational social agenda that, in their different ways, they were both devoted to.

In 1973, Chermayeff was awarded the Gold Medal of the Royal Architectural Institute of Canada, and, in his address at the ceremony he said,[21]

Whatever good I may have done could never have been done without my many students from all over the world. For many years we have collaborated in speculation about purposes and priorities. Research is not yet a term which can properly be applied in architecture. We worked together on a search for reasonable questions, which might lead to viable answers. Anyway, we learned to mistrust easy answers to problems without precedent. We tried to apply ourselves to issues and to let beauty look after herself, in the words of my old friend and mentor, Eric Gill.

This was closely paralleled by Leslie Martin, when he received the Royal Hold Medal for Architecture from the RIBA, also in 1973,[22]

I know of no other university subject in which students need not start by acquiring a body of knowledge. Architecture is potentially a very complete educational process because it requires students to learn by recognising problems, by identifying them, by analysing and evaluating their various parts, and then bringing everything together in final solutions. Moreover, in doing all this, students can take part in a collective effort in which comparative analysis becomes possible. It is the work of my students, more than anything else, that has widened my understanding of the range of the subject. And when I have seen it developed by special studies at an advanced level, I am astonished by the skill and capacity that is being developed at every level.

Notes

1 This essay was first published in *Architectural Research Quarterly*, Volume 5, No. 3, 2001, pp. 205–209.
2 J.L. Martin, Ben Nicholson, and Naum Gabo (Eds.), *Circle: International Survey of Constructive Art*, London, Faber & Faber, 1937, reprinted 1971. The contributors to this important document included painters – Braque, Duchamp, Kandinsky, Klee, Mondrian and Picasso; sculptors – Brancusi, Giacometti, Hepworth, Moore and Tatlin; architects – Aalto, Breuer, Le Corbusier, Gropius, Lubetkin, Mendelsohn and Neutra; and writers – Bernal, Giedion, Moholy-Nagy, Mumford, Read and Shand.
3 Christopher Alexander, *Notes on the Synthesis of Form*, Cambridge, MA, Harvard University Press, 1967.
4 Leslie Martin and Colin Buchanan, *Whitehall: A Plan for the National and Government Centre*, London, HMSO, 1965.
5 In 1974, March became professor of Systems Design at the University of Waterloo, returning to Britain in 1976 as professor of Design at the Open University and became provost of the Royal College of Art in 1981. Thereafter, he returned to the United States and remained at UCLA until his retirement and return to Britain in 2004.
6 Serge Chermayeff and Christopher Alexander, *Community and Privacy: Towards a New Architecture of Humanism*, New York, Doubleday & Co, 1963, Harmondsworth, Pelican Books, 1966.

7 Serge Chermayeff, in Richard Pluntz (Ed.), *Design and the Public Good*, Cambridge, MA & London, MIT Press, 1981.

8 Ibid.

9 Leslie Martin, 'Report on the Oxford Conference', *Journal of the Royal Institute of British Architects*, June 1958.

10 Serge Chermayeff, 'Memorandum to Josep-Lluís Sert, 5 November 1953', in *Chermayeff Papers*, SC Box 6 (55–59), (1955), Avery Library, Columbia University, New York.

11 Serge Chermayeff, 'Docket for the faculty meeting in the last week of April', in *Chermayeff Papers*, SC Box 6, (55–59), (1955), Avery Library, Columbia University, New York.

12 Serge Chermayeff, 'Suggested draft for the advanced studies fellowship program at the School of Architecture', in *Chermayeff Papers*, Avery Library, Columbia University, New York.

13 Give reference to some of these – Eisenman, Taylor, Croghan

14 Leslie Martin and Lionel March, 'Land use and built forms', *Cambridge Research*, April 1966.

15 See Essay 4 for further detail on these projects and the individuals involved.

16 Leslie Martin and Lionel March (eds.), *Urban Space and Structures*, Cambridge, UK, Cambridge University Press, 1972.

17 Leslie Martin, 'Architect's approach to architecture', *Journal of the Royal Institute of British Architects*, May 1967.

18 Alan Powers, *Serge Chermayeff: Designer, Architect, Teacher*, London, RIBA Publications, 2001.

19 Amongst these were Colin St. J Wilson, John Miller, Douglas Lanham and David Owers.

20 This is described in, David Croghan, 'The design of an artificial sky', *The Architects' Journal*, 22nd July 1964.

21 Serge Chermayeff, in Richard Pluntz (ed.), op cit.

22 Leslie Martin, 'The Bridges between the Cultures: The Royal Gold Medal in Architecture Address', *Journal of the Royal Institute of British Architects*, Volume 80, 1973.

Essay 4[1]
Bridging the cultures
Architecture, models and computers in 1960s Cambridge

Introduction

In 1956, Sir Leslie Martin was appointed the first Professor of Architecture at the University of Cambridge. There he began the transformation of the Cambridge Department of Architecture and, in a wider context, of architectural education in Britain. This essay charts these events and places particular emphasis in the work undertaken at the centre for Land Use and Built Form Studies (LUBFS), later to become the Martin Centre for Architectural and Urban Studies, in the period between its foundation in 1967 and Martin's retirement from the university in 1972. It was then that architectural studies benefitted from and participated in the interconnected themes of conceptual modelling and computer applications that were being widely explored in the university.

Early in his career, Martin made distinguished contributions to architectural education and practice in Britain. He was appointed head of the Hull School of Architecture in 1934, at the age of 26, and held the post until 1939. During the Hull years, Martin was joint editor with Ben Nicholson and Naum Gabo, of *Circle: International Survey of Constructive Art*.[2] In this they brought together a remarkable collection of contributors from a brilliant array of painters, sculptors, architects and writers. In 1939, Martin moved to London to join the Architects' Department of the London Midland and Scottish Railway from where he moved in the post-war years to the London County Council to lead the team that designed the Royal Festival Hall, the centrepiece of the Festival of Britain in 1951. He succeeded Robert Matthew as chief architect at the LCC in 1953 and consolidated the reputation of the Architects' Department as one of the leading design offices of the post-war years.

In 1958, the Royal Institute of British Architects (RIBA) held a conference at Magdalen College, Oxford, to discuss the current state and future development of architectural education in Britain.[3] It was the first time the profession had held a formal discussion on the subject of education since the International Congress in London in 1924. Fifty carefully selected delegates attended the conference. These came from home and abroad and

DOI: 10.4324/9781003083023-5

from both education and the profession. Just three sessions were held to discuss, respectively,

1. The needs of the profession and the community and the desirable standards;
2. The means of education, the routes of entry into the profession and the standards that are and could be achieved;
3. Developments of advanced training and research.

By all accounts, Martin was one of the most influential contributors to the conference and, significantly, he was the author of the conference report published in the *RIBA Journal*. This covers all three of the session topics, but it is the third, on *research*, that has proved to have the greatest influence on subsequent events and which has particular bearing on the subject of the present essay. The following extracts from the report convey the core of Martin's arguments on research.

> The advancement of knowledge is not merely an ornament to a profession – it is its duty. This is the means by which the competence of the profession as a whole can be advanced. It is essential to improvement that a limited number of people should at some time devote themselves to advanced post-graduate study and research.
>
> The evolution of post-graduate studies ... is a natural extension of higher standards of training within the schools. These studies are the means by which students of diversified interests extend their own minds and the boundaries of knowledge.
>
> Research is the tool by which theory is advanced. Without it teaching can have no direction and thought no cutting edge. Without theory research is no more than a study of techniques and parcels of this or that form of knowledge.[4]

In the decade following his arrival in Cambridge, Martin established his home and practice in the King's Mill at Great Shelford, four miles from the Department of Architecture. There he and his associates produced designs for a series of important buildings.[5] Slowly these projects began to benefit from the work of the Department's small band of post-graduate students. One of the most important of these was David Croghan, who was working on daylight design and, as a central part of his PhD project, designed and constructed a large 'Skydome', an instrument for measuring daylight in models of buildings, in the garden at the rear of the Department.[6] Working in association with Martin's office, Croghan contributed daylighting assistance on projects such as the Manor Road Libraries at Oxford, 1960–1964 and the University Zoology and Psychology Laboratories, also at Oxford, 1963–1971. He also contributed to the daylighting design of the extension to the Department of Architecture that was built in 1957–1959 to the design of Colin St John Wilson and Alex

Hardy.[7] This period saw a small increase in the number of PhD students in Architecture at Cambridge, who worked on a range of topics in history, theory and building science.[8] The most significant event, however, occurred in 1967, when Martin obtained three externally funded research grants to fund research teams to work on complementary projects covering distinct, but interconnected scales of enquiry. These were, in ascending physical scale: the *Offices Study* at the scale of the individual building, the *Universities Study*, where the focus was on the physical accommodation of a large, complex public institution and, finally, the *Urban Systems Study* in which the focus was on the entire city. Thus began the centre for Land Use and Built Form Studies, and the work moved into new methodological territory.

Background: models and computers

The background to the work of LUBFS was implicitly set out by Martin in a paper he delivered at the RIBA in January 1967 that was later published in full in the *RIBA Journal*.[9] Taking his cue from Alfred North Whitehead[10] and the distinction he drew between *practical* and *speculative* reason, Martin argued that in architecture, 'the rational understanding of a problem and the extension of this into speculative (intuitive) thought is one single process: that is, that thought and intuition are not opposed, but complementary'.

In his concluding paragraph Martin made, in my view, a key statement in relation to the future work of LUBFS:

> The ultimate problem for the profession is that of setting out the possibilities and choices in building an environment. And in that field the crisis will not be solved by technical advance alone or by picturesque images. At bottom it is a crisis of lack of understanding. Our task is to try to make that understanding more complete.

Armed with these broad principles and with the funding from three research grants, Martin gathered a group of young researchers all of whom, including the present author, were architecture graduates.[11] There was no precedent for a research undertaking of this scale in architecture. The earlier work in history, theory and building science was undertaken by 'lone scholars' using the methods of the humanities and applied science, but the new tasks required a completely different approach. In reviewing the situation that confronted us, Philip Steadman, one of the founder–members of LUBFS, has described how, as a student in the Department between 1960 and 1965, he experienced 'an orthodox Modernism, mingled with some remnants of Beaux Arts methods'. He also recalls being taught in the design studios by Colin St John (Sandy) Wilson, Colin Rowe and Peter Eisenman. He refers to the 'intellectual ferment (in the wider university) around mathematical modelling in the social sciences ... and, of crucial importance, the availability of the University's "Titan" mainframe computer'.[12]

As we began our work in 1967, a number of books by distinguished Cambridge scholars from across the disciplines were identifying the potential of 'models' as tools in research. Mary Hesse, from the Department of the History of Science, published an elegant 'slim volume', *Models and Analogies in Science*.[13] From Economics came Richard Stone's *Mathematics in the Social Sciences and Other Essays*[14] and Richard Chorley of the Department of Geography, in collaboration with Peter Haggett of the University of Bristol, co-edited *Models in Geography*.[15] A further interdisciplinary inspiration came from David Clarke's *Analytical Archaeology*.[16] Hesse's book was concerned with the debate between two conceptions of the world in the execution of science, the *abstract and systematic* versus the *Mechanical*. This was distant from our more pragmatic objectives in architecture and urbanism but provided intellectual stimulus and encouragement in finding a way forward. Stone's writings reinforced the idea that systematic methods had validity across the disciplines and Chorley and Hagget's collection of essays on the use of models in Geography came closer to our territory. Of particular value was the editors' joint introductory essay, 'Models and Paradigms in the New Geography', in which they reviewed terminology and definitions across what was already a well-established field. Of particular help were clarifications such as

> a model can be a theory or a law or a hypothesis or a structured idea. It can also be a synthesis of data. Most important from the geographical viewpoint, it can also include reasoning about the real world by means of translations in space (to give spatial models) or in time (to give historical models).[17]

Also, in the fertile year of 1967, the distinguished biologist turned philosopher of science, P.B. Medawar, published a collection of essays, *The Art of the Soluble*.[18] The last two of these essays seemed to me to be particularly relevant, 'Two Conceptions of Science' and 'Hypothesis and Imagination'. Both touched upon the question of the relation between *practical* and *speculative* reason that Leslie Martin had broached in his RIBA lecture. I was, and remain, struck by the following statement from the first of these essays:

> The factual burden of a science varies inversely with its degree of maturity. As a science advances, particular facts are comprehended within, and therefore in a sense annihilated by general statements of steadily increasing explanatory power and compass – whereupon then acts need no longer be known explicitly, i.e. spelled out and kept in mind. In all sciences we are being progressively relieved of the burden of singular instances, the tyranny of the particular. We need no longer record the fall of every apple.

In contrast to the fragmentary state of previous research in architecture, what Martin described at the Oxford Conference as, 'parcels of this or that form of knowledge', all-encompassing statements such as this hinted at a way forward.

The other significant influence on our work was the availability in Cambridge of a large mainframe computer. The background to this began in 1937, with the foundation, under the direction of Professor J.E. Lennard-Jones, of the Cambridge Mathematical Laboratory, which was renamed the Computer Laboratory in 1970. The aim was to provide computers to serve the needs of the University. Following World War II, during which the Laboratory worked under the Ministry of Supply, it returned to its original work with Maurice V. Wilkes appointed acting director in 1946. The Laboratory built its first computer, EDSAC (Electronic Delay Storage Automatic Calculator) that first ran a program in May 1946. Throughout the 1950s this machine was widely used by science departments in the University and was replaced in 1958 by a much-improved machine, EDSAC II. In 1964, this was in turn superseded by a greatly more powerful machine, 'Titan'.[19] This was housed in a Victorian building in Corn Exchange Street on the edge of the New Museums Site of science departments, amongst which was the Cavendish Laboratory of the Department of Physics. The machine occupied a large, air-conditioned room and was attended by a 'priesthood' of white-coated technicians. In March 1967, the Laboratory made the first experimental runs of an on-line, multiple-access system for 'Titan' that allowed simultaneous access to the machine by a number of users.[20] This became fully operational, with 64 remote terminals made available throughout the University, just as the founders of LUBFS were making their first, tentative steps into computing.

LUBFS – the founding studies

Before describing the work of the three founding studies at LUBFS, the origin of the title should be explained. It derives from the background research carried out by Leslie Martin and Lionel March in studies for the redevelopment of the Whitehall district of London as the centre of national government.[21] In these the properties of three distinct forms of development – 'built forms' – were evaluated. These were defined as *pavilions*, *streets* and *courts*. The studies revealed that the court form offers greater land use efficiency, *density*, than a tower. In 1966, the studies were published as, 'Land Use and Built Form Studies', in the journal *Cambridge Research*,[22] thus defining the overall identity of the new centre.

The three inaugural projects that allowed LUBFS to come into being, *Offices*, *Universities* and *Urban Systems*, respectively, represented a continuum of scale from the individual building as an element of the city, to the public institution and its accommodation, to the city as a whole. This invested the work with a degree of overall coherence, which was reinforced by the shared interest across the group in the potential of models in defining conceptual frameworks across all scales of investigation and the possibilities that were offered by applying the computer to these problems.

The nature of the original work may best be represented by the systems diagrams of the various models developed by the three studies. The Urban Systems Study had valuable precedent in work from North American scholars, particularly that of I.S. Lowry, whose 1964 model of Pittsburgh was an acknowledged point of departure.[23] At its core, this model represented the interaction of activities and the building stock of a city in its simple form in a clear diagram. A more complex representation was given in an elegant flow diagram published in a paper, 'A structural comparison of three generations of New Towns'.[24] This presented the results of a complex analysis, made by running the model on 'Titan', of the implications of the different spatial characteristics of four English towns: Reading, Stevenage, Hook and Milton Keynes. A project of this scope would have been inconceivable without such computing power.

The Universities Study worked at the scale of the 'urban sub-system', which they defined as, 'the grouping of activities and buildings that are built up around the developing universities'.[25] In the first stages of this project, the team proposed a comprehensive conceptual model of the sub-system as it related to university planning.[26] This identified three distinct categories of information, *The wider context*, *Population* and *Building type* and indicated connections or relationships between a complex of parameters within each. This was, perhaps, the most ambitious such representation to be produced in the early days of LUBFS. The model was never fully implemented as a computer model, but a number of what may be described as 'sub-models', conceived within the overall structure, were constructed, programmed and run on 'Titan'. One of these was a model that simulated day-to-day activities within a university. This was based on precedents of stochastic modelling, most from North America. A working example simulated the activities of a 10% sample of the students of a university of 3000 students as they moved between a number of locations over a 24-hour period.[27]

The work of the Offices Study focussed on two different aspects of the design of this building type. First was the analysis of route patterns in large buildings, 'Traffic in Buildings'. The second was analysis of the environmental performance of similar buildings. Philp Tabor undertook the former work. He began by making a comprehensive review of the emerging literature on the application of computer models in the planning of buildings, for example, the work of Whitehead and Eldars and of Beaumont.[28] He then executed an extensive series of modelling studies, using 'Titan', in which he evaluated the circulation patterns in alternative building plans, each with the same floor area.[29] In this work he was joined by Richard Stibbs, who had joined LUBFS from the Mathematical Laboratory and played a key role in the work of the Offices Study and of the wider group. The environmental studies that I initiated had their basis in the physics of heat, light and sound as this related to the performance of buildings. Much of the fundamental research originated at the

Building Research Station, a government-funded research institute, which had strong groups working across the field of building physics.[30] The outcome of this work was the Cambridge Environmental Model, a large scale computer model that ran on 'Titan' and incorporated a model of the form and construction of buildings and their immediate surroundings, a file of climate data and a series of algorithms that calculated quantities of heat, light and sound within the building and of energy consumption totals for all the seasons of the year.[31] The general structure of the model was indicated in the generic flow chart supplemented by an array of 'sub-models'.

Postscript

Looking back at this work after half a century, I am struck, perhaps even surprised, by the boldness with which we young architects plunged into the uncharted waters of models and computers. As Philip Steadman has observed, we were all the products of an architectural education, whether in Cambridge or elsewhere, which conformed to the general pattern that centred on the design studio, supplemented by courses in the history of architecture, building technology and professional practice. But, in the special circumstances that emerged in 1960s Cambridge, we embraced ideas and tools that were seemingly unrelated to that background. In my view and experience, the enthusiasm and leadership of Lionel March, both mathematician and architect, and formally designated as director of LUBFS, provided the day-to-day stimulus. He inspired us to read the books and to attend classes on computer programming in the strange and wonderful world of the Mathematical Laboratory. In just a small instance of the atmosphere in which we worked, I recall hurrying to show him the computer print-out – no computer graphics and screens in those days – on the morning when my algorithm that calculated the shadows cast across the façade of a building ran successfully for the first time. He shared in my delight at this now seemingly simple achievement, but what was then a great step towards the application of the computer in architecture.

But standing behind all of this was the presence of Leslie Martin. His influence, following his appointment at Cambridge in 1956 and his contribution to the Oxford Conference of 1958, established the platform from which research could move on from its previously sparse and fragmentary state. In 1973, the year after his retirement from the Department, Martin was awarded the Royal Gold Medal for Architecture by the RIBA. His address at the award ceremony on 12 June 1973 had the title, 'The bridges between the cultures'. In concluding this wide-ranging review of his life's work as practitioner and academic, Martin turned to this fundamental question of architectural education:

> I know of no other university subject in which students need not start by acquiring a body of knowledge. Architecture is potentially a very complete educational process because it requires students to learn by

recognising problems, by identifying them, by analysing and evaluating their various parts, and then bringing everything together in final solutions. Moreover, in doing this, students can take part in a collective effort in which comparative analysis becomes possible. It is the work of my students, more than anything else, that has widened my understanding of the range of our subject. And when I have seen it developed by special studies at an advanced level, I am astonished by the skill and capacity that is being developed at every level.

In 1974, LUBFS was renamed the Martin Centre for Architectural and Urban Studies. This was in part in recognition of the immense contribution Martin had made to the Department but was also an acknowledgement that the research was expanding into new areas of study that reached beyond the original terms of reference. Fifty years on, the Martin Centre has over 70 researchers of whom 30 are PhD students. The work ranges in subjects from History/Theory to Sustainable Building and Cities and Transport. This marks the fulfilment of those tentative beginnings in 1967. Architecture has become a mature discipline. To return to P.B. Medawar's inspiring essay, we need no longer count the fall of every apple.

Notes

1 This essay was first published in *Interdisciplinary Science Reviews*, Volume 42, Nos. 1–2, 2017, pp. 144–159.
2 J.L. Martin, Ben Nicolson, and N. Gabo, *Circle: International Survey of Constructive Art*, London, Gaber & Faber, 1937, Reprinted 1971.
3 J.L. Martin, 'Oxford Conference on Architectural Education', *Journal of the Royal Institute of British Architects*, Volume 65, June 1958.
4 Ibid.
5 The scope of Martin's practice throughout his career is described in Leslie Martin, *Buildings and Ideas 1933–83: From the Studio of Leslie Martin and His Associates*, Cambridge, Cambridge University Press, 1983.
6 David Croghan, 'The Design of an Artificial Sky', *The Architects' Journal*, 1964.
7 David Croghan, *Daylighting by Design: Some Early Examples of the Use of an Artificial Sky*, Cambridge, 2015 (unpublished text).
8 Among these was Peter Eisenman, who taught in the Department and was awarded his PhD for his dissertation, *The Formal Basis of Modern Architecture*, which was supervised by Leslie Martin, in 1964. The thesis was published in facsimile by Lars Müller, Publishers, Zurich, 2006.
9 Leslie Martin, 'Architect's Approach to Architecture', *Journal of the Royal Institute of British Architects*, May 1967.
10 Alfred North Whitehead, *The Function of Reason*, Princeton, NJ, Princeton University Press, 1929.
11 They were: Lionel March, who read both Mathematics and Architecture at Cambridge and four other Cambridge Architecture graduates, Nicholas Bullock, Peter Dickens, Philip Steadman and Philip Tabor plus Marcial Echenique, who had studied Architecture at Santiago, Chile and Barcelona and, finally, Dean Hawkes, who had studied at the Manchester School of Art and came to

Cambridge in 1965 to join David Croghan on the daylighting research. These were soon joined by other key contributors including architects David Crowther and Walton Lindsey on the Urban Systems work and, crucially, computer scientists, Crispin Grey, Janet Tomlinson and Richard Stibbs, all from the Cambridge Mathematical Laboratory.

12 Philip Steadman, 'Research in Architecture and Urban Studies at Cambridge in the 1960s and 1970s: What Really Happened', *The Journal of Architecture*, Volume 21, No. 2, 2016, pp. 291–306.

13 Mary Hesse, *Models and Analogies in Science*, Indiana, University of Notre Dame Press, 1966.

14 Richard Stone, *Mathematics in the Social Sciences and Other Essays*, London, Chapman & Hall, 1966.

15 Richard Chorley and Peter Haggett, (Eds.), *Models in Geography*, London, Methuen & Co., 1967.

16 David Clarke, *Analytical Archaeology*, London, Methuen & Co., 1968.

17 Richard Chorley and Peter Haggett, op cit.

18 P.B. Medawar, *The Art of the Soluble*, London, Methuen & Co., 1967.

19 These events are described at length in Maurice V. Wilkes, *Memories of a Computer Pioneer*, Cambridge, MA, MIT Press, 1985.

20 Maurice V, Wilkes, 'The Cambridge Multiple-Access System in Retrospect', *Software Practice and Experience*, Volume 3, 1973, pp. 323–332.

21 Leslie Martin and Colin Buchanan, *Whitehall: A Plan for a National Government Centre*, London, HMSO, 1965.

22 Leslie Martin and Lionel March, 'Land Use and Built Forms', *Cambridge Research*, Volume 2, 1966.

23 David Crowther and Marcial Echenique, 'Development of a Model of Urban Space and Structure', in Leslie Martin and Lionel March (Eds.), *Urban Space and Structures*, Cambridge, Cambridge University Press, 1972.

24 Marcial Echenique, David Crowther, and Walton Lindsay, 'A Structural Comparison of Three Generations of New Towns', *Land Use and Built Form Studies. Working Paper no. 25*, Cambridge, University of Cambridge, 1969. Reprinted in Leslie Martin and Lionel March, *Urban Space and Structures*, op cit.

25 Nicholas Bullock, Peter Dickens, and Philip Steadman, 'The Modelling of Day-to-Day Activities', in Leslie Martin and Lionel March (Eds.), *Urban Space and Structures*, op cit.

26 Nicholas Bullock, Peter Dickens, and Philip Steadman, 'A Theoretical Basis for University Planning', *Land Use and Built Form Studies Report*, Cambridge, University of Cambridge, 1968. Reprinted in Leslie Martin and Lionel March, *Urban Space and Structures*, ibid.

27 Nicholas Bullock, Peter Dickens, and Philip Steadman, 'The Modelling of Day-to-Day Activities', in Leslie Martin and Lionel March (Eds.), *Urban Space and Structures*, ibid.

28 B. Whitehead and M.Z. Eldars, 'The Planning of Single-Storey Layouts', *Building Science*, Volume 1, 1965. M.J.S. Beaumont, *Computer Aided Techniques for the Synthesis of Layout and Form with Respect to Circulation*, unpublished thesis, Department of Engineering, University of Bristol, 1967.

29 Philip Tabor, 'Analysing Communication Patterns' and 'Analysing Route Patterns', in Lionel March (Ed.), *The Architecture of Form*, Cambridge, Cambridge University Press, 1976.

30 See F.M. Lea, *Science and Building: A History of the Building Research Station*, London, HMSO, 1971. Figures at BRS whose work was directly influential on the environmental work at LUBFS were: E. Danter for his work on periodic heat flow, R.G. Hopkinson and his group for their fundamental work on the

calculation of daylight in buildings and P.H. Parkin and H.R. Humphries for their work in acoustics.

31 Dean Hawkes, 'The Modelling of the Environmental Performance of Built Forms', in Lionel March (Ed.), *The Architecture of Form*, op cit., pp. 381–388.

Essay 5[1]
The environment of the Elizabethan house
Hardwick Hall

Introduction

Hardwick 'New' Hall was built between 1591 and 1599 and is one of the most important houses of Elizabethan England. It was the home of Elizabeth, Countess of Shrewsbury, familiarly referred to as 'Bess of Hardwick', and the work of the architect Robert Smythson (1536–1614). It stands on a hilltop and is immediately adjacent to the 'Old' Hall that was itself under construction between 1587 and 1598.[2] The appearance of the house is remarkable, with walls of local stone pierced by enormous mullioned windows and six turrets that rise high above the roofline (Figure 6.2). The exterior observes and dramatically demonstrates the principles of strict symmetry that were an important aspect of the architecture of the English renaissance, but this conceals a surprising asymmetry and complexity of interior organisation. Examination of the plans of the house shows how this organisation is founded on the observation of what we may now recognise to be principles of environmental design. This essay presents an environmental analysis of the house with particular emphasis on the conditions of Bess' personal first floor apartments, as they might have been experienced when they were occupied by Bess between 4 October 1597, when she moved into the house, until her death there on 13 January 1608.

In providing shelter for their occupants, buildings mediate between the variable and unpredictable external climate and the desire for more constant and moderate conditions within. To understand a house constructed four centuries ago we must, therefore, construct a description of the climate of that time. It is then necessary to develop an understanding of the internal environment that would have been sought by the inhabitants of a great Elizabethan house. This leads to an analysis of the basic principles of organisation, construction and equipment of the house as these relate to its environmental qualities.

Climate and comfort in Elizabethan England

At the end of the sixteenth century, meteorology in its modern sense was unknown. Instruments for the measurement of temperature and

DOI: 10.4324/9781003083023-6

atmospheric pressure were yet to be developed.[3] But climate was keenly observed by other means and from these we may recreate a description of the conditions in which Hardwick was conceived and inhabited. The most notable fact to register is that at this date England was in the depths of the so-called Little Ice Age that extended from the fourteenth to the nineteenth centuries.[4] For the period 1580–1620 proxy records have been used to reconstruct descriptions of the conditions that were most probably experienced.[5] These indicate that England suffered from extremely cold winters with deep frosts and frequent snowfall, but also from warm summers and drought. The average annual temperature has been estimated to have been 1 degree Celsius below that of the late twentieth century and the winters considerably colder. It was under these conditions that Hardwick was built and its elderly owner lived in the house.

This was, of course, the time of Shakespeare (1554–1616) and vivid descriptions of contemporary climate may be found throughout his works. To contrast winter and summer we have

> When all aloud the wind doth blow,
> And coughing drowns the parson's saw;
> And birds sit brooding in the snow,
> And Marion's nose looks red and raw,

Love's Labour's Lost
Act V, Scene ii

> Shall I compare thee to a summer's day?
> Thou art more lovely and more temperate:
> Rough winds do shake the darling buds of May,
> And summer's lease hath all too short a date:
> Some times too hot the eye of heaven shines,
> And often is his gold complexion dimm'd;

The Sonnets, 18[6]

These capture the sense of the coldness of those Little Ice Age winters and periods of great summer heat tempered, then as now, in England by the unpredictability and brevity of our summers.

At a time when the environment within a building was more closely connected with the external climate than in our time, its occupants would have had a much keener perception of the annual cycle of the seasons and of the daily passing of the hours than our twenty-first-century experience, cushioned by elaborate environmental control systems. Comfort was perceived quite differently from our modern expectations. The Shakespeare scholar Jonathan Bate has emphasised how,

> In an age of candle and rush-light, nights were seriously dark. The night
> was accordingly imagined to be seriously different from the day. The

very fact of long hours of light itself conferred a kind of magic upon midsummer night.[7]

In developing an understanding of the environmental expectations and perceptions of the Elizabethans, we may infer a similar awareness of the thermal environment in which interiors were more responsive to external conditions. Indeed, we might assume that the experience of 'comfort' was complex and diverse, with activities expanding and contracting in time and space. This is the basis upon which we may examine the environment of Hardwick.

Hardwick described

The primary source for describing Hardwick is the house itself. Although four centuries old, its form and construction remain relatively unchanged.[8] Significant documentary sources are the Building Accounts[9] and the comprehensive Inventories of 1601,[10] compiled just four years after Bess first moved in.

The overall configuration of the plan is strikingly simple. It consists of a rectangle that is elaborated by the addition of six projecting turrets. A massive masonry spine wall runs the entire length, slightly offset from the long axis. This is most clearly seen at second floor level. The plan is oriented with its long axis close to the north-south cardinal. At the ground and first floors the double-height Hall subdivides the plan, defined by thick masonry walls. The complex detailed planning of the house is then superimposed upon this essentially simple diagram (Figure 5.1).

The accommodation is broadly arranged with servants' quarters at ground level, the principal family rooms on the first floor and the great rooms of state on the second floor. At the ground floor the north of the plan is principally occupied by the kitchens, large and small, and the associated buttery, scullery and larders. The only exception to these domestic places is the double-height Chapel, whose lower level occupies the north-east turret. To the south of the Hall lie the Pantry and a smaller, associated chamber. The remainder of this wing contains domestic apartments, including, significantly, the Nursery.

Before outlining the principal apartments of the upper floors, it is appropriate to discuss the building's two staircases. They are both on the east side of the house. The north stair winds a complex route to the first floor from where it enters the north turret to proceed to the second floor, giving access to the staterooms and then on to roof level. The south stair is a much grander, ceremonial event. It rises from the ground to the first floor in a generous dog-leg arrangement to arrive at a spacious landing at the entrance to the Countess of Shrewsbury's personal apartments. From there it proceeds southwards and terminates in a dramatic sweeping turn in the brightly lit

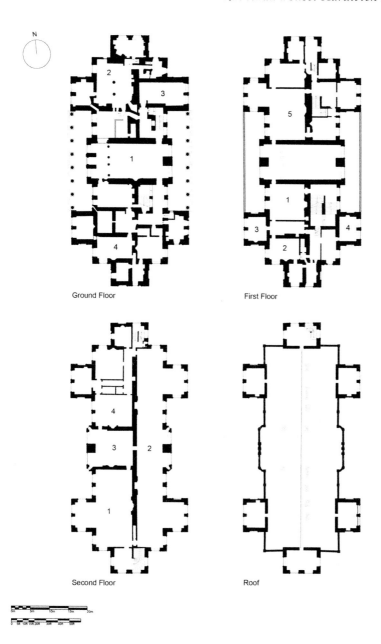

Figure 5.1 Hardwick Hall, floor plans. (Author: Dean Hawkes)

south turret at the entrance to the High Great Chamber, the most significant room in the house.

Returning to the internal planning of the house, the first floor is divided into north and south parts by the double-height volume of the Hall. The whole of the south end is occupied by Bess' personal apartments and those of the closest members of the household. These rooms will be the subjects of detailed discussion later. To the north of the hall is the Low Great Chamber, a magnificent formal room, and the Little Dining Chamber, both conveniently placed above the kitchens. The second floor houses the most important ceremonial rooms of the house. Arriving from the long, elaborate progress of the main stair, the point of arrival is the magnificently decorated High Great Chamber. This measures 19.75 metres in length and between 9.75 and 15.00 metres in width. It occupies the entire the south-west corner. Immediately by the entrance, a door leads into the Long Gallery, which, at 61 metres, extends the full length of the east side of the plan. The remainder of this floor, the Withdrawing Chamber, Best Bedchamber and other associated chambers, constituted in effect a state suite, which it has been surmised, was created in anticipation of a visit by the Queen.[11] Above these rooms is an attic storey, accessed by the north stair that reduces their ceiling height. This originally did not cover the Withdrawing Chamber, but was extended over that at some date before 1764[12], reducing its height. Finally, the north stair arrives at roof level in the north turret from where access is made to the roof, the 'leads' in contemporary usage. In the sixteenth and seventeenth centuries, these were commonly used for outdoor exercise and other recreations.

Fireplaces and windows

The twentieth-century British architect Peter Smithson wrote of Hardwick, 'What's nice about [the plan] is that it indicates the thick spine wall, where the fireplaces are ... and the perimeter bay windows that let in the light'.[13] This is an elegant characterisation of the environmental essence of the house in which numerous fireplaces in the thermal mass of the masonry core compensate for the heat loss through the windows. If we exclude the four hearths in the roof turrets, the house as built had 31 fireplaces. The great windows are, perhaps, the most striking aspect of the appearance of the house, and it is said that early in its existence it acquired the soubriquet, 'Hardwick Hall, more glass than wall'. The High Great Chamber is the glassiest room of all with eight great windows, each consisting of 12 individual lights. But elsewhere, appearances can be deceptive, and careful examination shows that no less than 30 of the windows, in a total of 156, approximately 19 per cent, were constructed 'blind' over inner masonry walls.[14] In the detailed analysis that follows it is proposed that these arrangements were not arbitrary, but were integral to the environmental logic that informed the entire design.

Orientation and insolation

A key factor in environmental analysis is the relationship between a building and the sun's passage across the sky. As a universal constant, this has not changed between the sixteenth century and the present. Hardwick stands at the latitude of 53 degrees and 10 minutes north and longitude of 1 degree and 19 minutes west. Its elevation is 151 metres above sea level. At the date of Hardwick's construction, life was regulated by sun time as it was observed at each location. At Hardwick the key factors may be summarized as follows (Table 5.1).

People living at the end of the sixteenth century would have been deeply aware of the facts represented by the sun path diagram and the table below. In a largely agrarian society, much of their life was spent out of doors, and buildings, by their nature, admitted a sense of daily and seasonal cycles to their interiors.

The orientation of the long axis of Hardwick is offset just 6 degrees to the east of due north. If the plan is superimposed on the polar sun path diagram we may observe how orientation informs the planning of the building (Figure 5.2). The benefit to the southerly rooms is immediately apparent. At the ground floor, the nursery is in a particularly advantageous place at the south-west corner with windows in adjacent south and west-facing walls. Alternatively, the location of the kitchens and larders at the north end of the house is clearly practical in providing cool storage and preventing solar warmth from exaggerating the heat of the cooking fires. At the first floor, the entire southern end of the house is devoted to Bess' own apartments and those of her closest family and servants.

The second floor contains the great ceremonial and staterooms and is the most luminous part of the house. The High Great Chamber (Figure 5.3) was the site of feasts and entertainments, and its location and organisation are finely calibrated to provide the best setting for these events. This magnificently decorated room is where the principal meals of dinner and supper were served, in direct response to the constraints of available natural

Table 5.1 Solar Data for Hardwick, Latitude 53° 10' N

		Winter Solstice	*Autumnal & Vernal Equinox*	*Summer Solstice*
Sunrise				
	Time (GMT)	08.20	06.00	03.40
	Azimuth	132°	180°	48°
Sunset				
	Time	15.40	18.00	20.20
	Azimuth	228°	270°	312°
Altitude at Noon	13°		37°	60°

Data compiled by author.

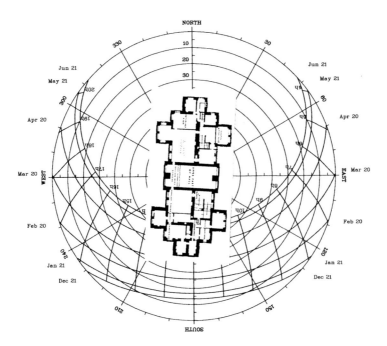

Figure 5.2 Hardwick Hall, Plan superimposed on polar sun path diagram. (Author: Dean Hawkes)

light, at late morning and afternoon respectively.[15] This is the most highly glazed room in the house and, in the summer months, would be flooded with light from midday until sunset as the sun moved towards the west. The Inventory of 1601[16] does not mention the presence of any curtains at the windows of the room, so its brightness would have been undiminished. Nor is there mention of any fixed or permanent source of night-time illumination. The Inventories tell that the Great Hall had fixed candlesticks and others were kept nearby in the Pantry and Buttery. This suggests that the High Great Chamber would have been lit by some of the twenty-five portable candlesticks that were identified as kept in the Porter's Lodge. The contrast between summer and winter would have been extreme. The sole heat source is the magnificent fireplace set in the spine wall, equipped with, as the Inventories list, 'a payre of brass andyrons, a fier shovel, a payre of tonges'. The presence of 'andyrons' indicates that the fuel burned was wood, and we may conclude that the fireplace brought relatively little comfort to the room on a cold winter's evening. This probably encouraged the household to retreat early to smaller, more congenial places. There is some evidence that great rooms at this period were differently decorated according to the season, and Thornton[17] has pointed out that the Hardwick Inventories refer to two pairs of 'hanginges' for the High Great Chamber, one of tapestry the

Figure 5.3 Hardwick Hall, High Great Chamber. (National Trust Images/Nick Guttridge)

other of woollen cloth. The former still hang in the room, the latter have disappeared. If they were ever in use, the room would have had a very different atmosphere according to the season.

The Long Gallery (Figure 5.4) occupies the length of the east side of the second floor. This was where Bess and other senior members of the household took daily exercise, most particularly in inclement weather. The easterly orientation makes this an ideal place to be in the morning. In comparison with the High Great Chamber not all of the windows are glazed. The two north-facing lights in the turrets are blind[18] providing these spaces with just east and south light and excluding the disadvantageous north aspect. The walls of the gallery are faced with a set of tapestries, illustrating the biblical story of Gideon and the Midianities, bought by Bess in 1592. They remain in situ to the present day. The room was quite sparsely furnished, but was notable for the number of cushions, some specifically placed in the window bays. This suggests that these were attractive places to sit on sunny mornings. Again, no curtains are mentioned in the Inventories. There are two fireplaces in the spine wall, comparable with that of the High Great Chamber. These were also equipped with andirons, a fire shovel and tongs. They are located in the narrow part of the gallery, not opposite the window bays. This would help them to provide

Figure 5.4 Hardwick Hall, Long Gallery. (National Trust Images/Nick Guttridge)

a small field of warmth within the vast space, to allow a walker to pause for some comfort as she traversed the gallery on a cold day. There is an account of an event that took place on 7 January 1603 that suggests that the Gallery had an at least tolerable environment in the depths of winter. Sir Henry Bronker, a commissioner sent by the Queen, came, apparently unannounced, and recorded,

> I arrived at Hardwick and found the house without strange company. My Lady of Shrewsbury after she had my name, sent for me in her gallery where she was walking with La: Arbella (Bess' granddaughter) and her son William Cavendish.[19]

The accommodation of the second floor is completed by a suite of sumptuous bedrooms that were intended for the most important visitors.

Finally, the rooftop 'leads' were, in effect, a great outdoor room. When weather permitted, they would be used for exercise, and other recreations and entertainments would take place there in the summer months. The roof turrets could play a part in these. The four turrets oriented east and west have fireplaces and could thus offer additional comfort. The south turret is given special significance by Bess' arms above the entrance. This does not have a fireplace, but is glazed to east, west and south and becomes, in effect, a solarium on sunny days.

Bess' apartments – a house within a house

The first floor of the house is protected from the elements by the floors below and above and is the location of the most intensively occupied rooms. To the north of the double-height volume of the Hall is the Low Great Chamber, the largest of the apartments, 13.00 metres long and between 9.75 and 14.75 metres wide, with the fully glazed turret almost a room in itself measuring 6.00 by 5.00 metres. This was lavishly furnished and decorated as a setting for dining and recreation by the household. To the south and connected by a gallery above the Hall were Bess' most intimate apartments, which also housed her closest family members and companions. These are especially significant in a study of the historic environment. Their significance is declared by the entrance to Bess' Withdrawing Chamber that opens from the wide landing of the great stair. This is brightly lit from the east by two large windows. The entrance door is surmounted by a plaster cartouche that presents the head of a soldier set in a deep frame to declare the significance of the apartment.

The Withdrawing Chamber itself (Figure 5.5) is 9.75 metres deep and 9.25 metres wide. The floor to ceiling height, as throughout this floor, is 4.5 metres. The fireplace is on the inner wall and there are two, west-facing windows, each of nine lights. Although a relatively private place, accessible only to the closest family members and servants, this was a key room in the house, and the comfort of its principal occupant would have been a priority. The 1601 Inventory lists a number of seats with 'a chayre of black lether guilded, a footstoole of wood, a foot turkie Carpet'. This is clearly Bess' own chair, with the added comfort of the carpet-covered footstool. Two other chairs are listed, plus, 'too Chares for Children', eleven 'Stooles' of various material and a number of 'forms' and numerous cushions of fine material. Other items including a cupboard and various chests providing storage for small items. There was also an 'inlayed borde', a table that was, as was the practice, covered by carpets. The principal decoration was six hanging tapestries that survive to the present day. The fireplace is described as, 'an Iron Chymney, with a back of Iron' its surround displays the Hardwick arms. There were the usual andirons, fire tongs and shovel. The Inventory also lists three 'skreynes'. At this date this could refer to either a large folding screen that would be used to define a small area within a room, or it could be a smaller free-standing item that was used to provide protection from the heat of a fire.[20] It is likely that the three referred to here were of the latter kind and were used to protect the faces of the occupants of the three chairs as they sat by the fire.

As the sun path diagram shows, the west-facing windows do not admit sunlight in the winter months, as they are obstructed by the projecting

Figure 5.5 Hardwick Hall, Withdrawing Chamber. (National Trust Images/Andreas von Einsiedel)

turret, but are bright from mid-afternoon until sunset throughout the summer months. Unlike the great public rooms on the second floor, these windows were curtained, 'too Curtins of darnix'.[21] This was, most probably, to provide some thermal protection on winter evenings. In a room of this size there are distinct 'environmental zones' with different lighting and thermal conditions, dependent on the season and time of day. The relatively high ceiling and the clear view of the sky allow daylight to reach deep into the room. On a bright summer's afternoon, the area close to the windows would be particularly pleasant, warm and bright. In winter, on the other hand, the reach of heat from the fire would extend only a short distance and the useable space would contract to the inner part of the room. Thermal comfort would also be associated with dim light. On lighting at this time, Thornton observes, 'It is difficult for us to conceive how little light there normally was ... after dark. ... In fact, the strongest light in a room after dark would mostly come from the fire'.[22]

Bess' Bed Chamber was the most intimate and complex environment in the house. Thornton describes the efforts that were made to provide protection against the cold of the Little Ice Age by the layers of curtains to the windows and enclosing her bed, along with the depths of covers upon it and carpets on the floor.[23] The room, which measures 7.75 metres by 5.50 metres, is deeply embedded into the body of the house. Its only external surfaces are the two walls containing the west- and south-facing windows. These provide ample daylight. The fireplace is in the south wall adjacent to the window. This arrangement ensures that the room is highly protected against the elements. In addition to listing numbers of chairs, stools, writing desks and chests, the Inventory records that 'My Ladie Arbells bedsted' was also in the room, although she also had a personal chamber nearby. The arrangement of all of these items is not clear, not least the position of the beds. It is probable that these were in the inner part of the room and that the daytime activities took place at the southwest corner. Thus, the bed chamber received the best of afternoon sunlight at all seasons and in winter was also within reach of the warmth of the fire.

There is uncertainty regarding the exact use of the other rooms in Bess' group. The arrangement shown in the plan is based on that suggested by Durant and Riden.[24] This proposes that Arbella's chamber was in the southeast turret and describes the chamber in the southwest turret, that is entered from Bess' Withdrawing Chamber, as 'Chamber where my Lord's arms are', that may have been the apartment of Bess' son, William Cavendish. It is assumed that the rooms in the south turret were occupied by Bess' personal attendants and maids. All of these chambers have windows in just one wall, the others being blind, which is more appropriate to their dimensions and uses. Arbella's chamber in the southeast turret was furnished with damask and silk wall hangings and a canopied bed with curtains of silk and taffeta with ample mattresses, quilts and covers. There is no explicit reference to curtains, but the Inventory includes, 'ten pieces of Darnix', that might have served this purpose. In other respects, the room appears to have been quite sparsely furnished with only a cupboard, a square table and a stool, plus a number of cushions, suggesting Arbella spent more time elsewhere. The fireplace had the usual fire shovel and tonges. The Inventory suggests that William Cavendish's chamber in the southwest turret was also primarily used as a bedroom.

Conclusion

The aim of this essay has been to reach behind the striking appearance of Hardwick Hall to discover the environmental principles that, in some measure, inform its complex internal planning. One of the surprises and delights of the house is that the strict bi-axial symmetry of the exterior conceals an internal arrangement that is, on first encounter, of perplexing complexity. This is quite unlike the Italian works of his near contemporary, Andrea Palladio (1508–80), where exterior symmetry derived from exact internal symmetry, and differs even from Smythson's own earlier great house at Wollaton (1580–88). The reasons for this are most certainly many, but the analysis presented here suggests that what we now refer to as 'environmental' considerations were hugely influential.

The orientation of the building, with its long axis almost exactly on the north-south cardinal, establishes a fundamental differentiation between the environments of the spaces to north and south of the central Hall. Throughout the house, the orientation of the principal rooms may be interpreted by reference to their specific uses. The bright morning light of the Long Gallery and the flood of afternoon light into the High Great Chamber precisely accord with the times when they were the most used. Most convincing of all is the location and arrangement of Bess' personal apartments at the south of the first floor. Here they provide protection and comfort at all seasons for their elderly inhabitant and the closest members of her household. In addition, the analysis shows how the dramatic 'glassiness' of the exterior was quite precisely calibrated by the construction blind windows to fine-tune the environment of individual rooms.

In the late sixteenth century the notion of 'comfort' was certainly much different from our present expectations. But this study of Hardwick Hall helps to show that, in the depths of the Little Ice Age, it was possible for the architect and his remarkable client to reconcile the elaborate expression of status and rank and the highest ambitions of formal composition with subtle accommodation of human needs.

Acknowledgements

I should like to thank the following for their assistance with this project. Dr. Nigel Wright, Building and Collections Manager, The National Trust, Hardwick Hall, for allowing access to the house. Nigel Coote, Plowman Craven & Associates, Surveyors, Harpenden, for supplying the digital survey of Hardwick. Stan Finney, Department of Architecture, University of Cambridge, for help with CAD. Luke Kon, Darwin College, Cambridge, for drawing the digital plans.

Notes

1 This essay was first published in *Further Studies in the History of Construction*, Proceedings of the Third Annual Conference of the Construction History Society, Cambridge, 2016.

2 These building dates are from the Hardwick Building Accounts as published in David N. Durant and Philip Riden, *The Building of Hardwick Hall, Part 1: The Old Hall, 1587–91, Part 2: The New Hall, 1591–98*, Chesterfield, Derbyshire Record Society, Volume IV, 1980, Volume IX, 1984.

3 See W.E. Knowles Middleton, *Invention of the Meteorological Instruments*, Baltimore, MD, Johns Hopkins University Press, 1969.

4 Brian Fagan, *The Little Ice Age: How Climate Made History, 1300–1850*, New York, Basic Books, 2000.

5 See Mike Hulme, 'Climate', in Bruce R. Smith (Ed.), *The Cambridge Guide to the Worlds of Shakespeare*, Cambridge, Cambridge University Press, 2016.

6 Jonathan Bate and Eric Rasmussen (Eds.), *William Shakespeare: Complete Works*, London, The Royal Shakespeare Company/Macmillan, 2007.

7 Jonathan Bate, 'Introduction to a Midsummer Night's Dream', in Jonathan Bate and Eric Rasmussen (Eds.), *William Shakespeare: Complete Works*, op cit.

8 See Mark Girouard, *Robert Smythson and the Elizabethan Country House*, New Haven, CT, Yale University Press, 1983.

9 Durant, Riden, op cit.

10 Lindsay Boynton (Ed.), *The Hardwick Inventories of 1601*, London, The Furniture History Society, 1971.

11 See Mark Girouard, *Hardwick Hall*, London, The National Trust, 1989, revised edition 2002.

12 Girouard, ibid.

13 Peter Smithson, *Conversations with Students: A Space for Our Generation*, Catherine Spellman and Carl Unglaub (Eds.), New York, Princeton Architectural Press, 2005.

14 The numbers of fireplaces and blind windows are calculated from the detailed survey of the house carried out in 1998 by Messrs. Plowman, Craven Surveyors, Harpenden.

15 Girouard, op cit.

16 Boynton, *The Hardwick Inventories of 1601*, op cit.

17 Peter Thornton, *Seventeenth-Century Interior Decoration in England, France & Holland*, New Haven, CT & London: Yale University Press, 1981.

18 The opening in the southeast turret would appear to have been constructed 'blind', but the different construction of the closure of the opening in the north-east turret suggests this might have been a later alteration.

19 Cited in David N. Durant, *Bess of Hardwick: Portrait of an Elizabethan Dynast*, London, Peter Owen Publishers, revised edition, 1999. The original is in the Cecil Papers at Hatfield House

20 See Thornton, *Seventeenth-Century Interior Decoration in England, France and Holland*, op cit., for a discussion of fire screens.

21 'Darnix' was a woollen fabric used for curtains and wall hangings. From 'Doornick', the Flemish name for Tournai.

22 Thornton, Note 16.

23 Peter Thornton, 'A Short Commentary on the Hardwick Hall Inventory of 1601', in Boynton (Ed.), op cit.

24 Slightly different plans are offered by Boynton to accompany the 1601 Inventories (1971), Girouard in the National Trust Guidebook (1989) and Durant and Riden to accompany the Building Accounts (1984). The plan here is based on the last of these. This is also presented in David N. Durant, *The Smythson Circle: The Story of Six Great English Houses*, London, Peter Owen Publishers, 2011.

Essay 6[1]
The origins of building science in the architecture of Renaissance England

Introduction

In the twenty-first century, *building science* is a firmly established concept and plays an important role in the practice of architecture, in applied research and in architectural education. In its modern definition, the origins of building science can be traced back to the nineteenth century, in the wake of the industrial revolution, when it developed hand-in-hand with the new technologies of building: structure, construction, materials and heating and ventilation.[2] Joseph Gwilt's *Encyclopaedia of Architecture*, first published in 1825, was throughout the nineteenth century a major technical reference work for British architects.[3] The book is in four parts:

Book I, History of Architecture
Book II, Theory of Architecture
Book III, Practice of Architecture
Book IV, Valuation of Property

It is in Book II, 'Theory of Architecture' that we find the technical/scientific content with chapter discussions, such as:

Mathematics and Mechanics of Construction
Materials Used in Building
Use of Materials or Practical Building (this includes extensive sections on 'Ventilation' and 'Warming')

In the twentieth century, building science advanced and became institutionalised with the creation of publicly funded research organisations such as the Building Research Station (BRS) in Britain and the Reichsforschungsgesellschaft für Wirtschaftlichkeit im Bau und Wohnungswesen (RFG) in Germany.[4] Although the relationship between building science and the practice and theory of architecture has been largely uncharted – and, in many ways, is uncertain, elements of science and technology are central to the very nature of modern building.[5]

DOI: 10.4324/9781003083023-7

The relationship between architecture and science has, however, a much longer history. This essay examines how architecture was transformed by the emergence of organised science in England in the period between the end of the sixteenth century and the middle years of the eighteenth century. The discussion is principally concerned with the aspect of building design that we now identify as 'environmental' and focusses on three distinct phases in architectural history; the last years of the reign of Queen Elizabeth I, with the remarkable 'prodigy' houses built by Robert Smythson; the second part of the seventeenth century, when Christopher Wren emerged as the dominant figure in English architecture; and the middle years of the eighteenth century when the 'Palladian movement' adapted the sixteenth-century architecture of the Veneto to the English condition.

In the history of science, this period is referred to as the 'early modern era'. The introduction to Volume 3 of *The Cambridge History of Science* characterises it as a time of

> pell-mell change at every level: the astounding growth in the number of plant species and mathematical curves identified, for example, the creation of whole new ways of conceiving the natural order, such as the idea of 'natural law', the deployment of natural philosophers as technical experts on the government payroll and of natural philosophy as the best argument for religion.[6]

'The Mechanical Arts' of the sixteenth century embraced 'practical applications of mathematical knowledge in fields such as architecture, navigation, clockmaking and engineering'.[7] The invention of machines for a myriad of purposes was a great project of the period. J.A. Bennett has catalogued innovations made in the development of clocks and celestial instruments, mathematical and optical instruments and tools for navigation, surveying, warfare and cartography.[8] Many of these were relevant to and, in some instances, derived from architecture. Bennett also points to the important part played in this early science by the particularly architectural skill of drawing. In the seventeenth century, the science of meteorology came into being as instruments by which to measure the weather – atmospheric pressure, air temperature, the velocity and direction of the wind and rainfall – were devised and progressively refined.[9] The foundation of the Royal Society brought a new focus and organisation to the development of science in England. This took place on 28 November 1660, at a meeting held in Gresham College, London, following a lecture by Christopher Wren, who, at that time, was a scientist and Gresham professor of astronomy. He was, of course, to become the dominant architect of the age. In 1665, the Society established the *Philosophical Transactions*, which initiated the practice of authoritative publication of scientific work and was soon imitated throughout Europe.[10] Isaac Newton (1642–1727), the greatest scientist of the day, was elected a fellow of the Society in 1672 and became its president in

1701, a position he held until his death in 1727. Under the auspices of the Society and profound influence of Newton, English science flourished in the eighteenth century and entered a new relationship with both the theory and practice of architecture.

Architecture and science in the sixteenth century

In sixteenth-century England, both architecture and science were quite unlike their modern definitions and practices. Writing about the idea of the architect at this period, Mark Girouard suggests that,

> Although John Shute ... and John Dee ... expounded the Renaissance and Vitruvian ideal of the architect, the concept remained an alien one. The mediaeval system continued with little alteration.[11]

In contrast to this, Summerson describes England's most significant building organisation at the end of the sixteenth century, the Royal Works.[12] Located at a permanent building yard in Whitehall, the organisation was presided over by the surveyor, beneath whom was a hierarchy of subordinates who represented and supervised the work of large numbers of tradesmen, carpenters, joiners, masons and other trades. This provided the model by which most large building projects were undertaken and suggests that building practice for such projects had moved on from the informal procedures of earlier times.

Robert Smythson was responsible for some of the greatest buildings of Elizabethan England. Girouard surmises that he may have been born in the north of England and that he served an apprenticeship as a mason in London, when he would have learnt to draw. His memorial in the church at Wollaton near Nottingham describes him as, 'architector and survayor'.[13] It is drawing that allows us to identify Smythson as an architect. The Smythson Collection of the Royal Institute of British Architects preserves a large number of drawings definitively identified as drawn by him. Other drawings in the collection from the same period are in the hand of his architect son, Robert, and others.[14] Although some of the drawings are of measured surveys of existing buildings, others are clearly drawings made before the construction of buildings and, hence, illustrate the relationship between drawing and building that survives into modern practice. Smythson was, in that sense, an architect.

There are two great houses that most completely reveal Smythson's genius, Wollaton Hall near Nottingham (1580–1588) (Figure 6.1) and Hardwick Hall, Derbyshire (1590–1597) (Figure 6.2). These are counted among the 'Prodigy Houses', a group of country houses built by minsters and courtiers of Queen Elizabeth I.[15] Smythson was a near contemporary of Andrea Palladio, their dates being 1534–1614 and 1508–1580 respectively, but their buildings could hardly be more different. In contrast to the absolute classicism of Palladio's villas, these English houses barely reveal its

Figure 6.1 Robert Smythson, Wollaton Hall, from northeast. (Dean Hawkes)

influence. Summerson observes, 'Classicism made its way in England not as a method of building, but as a mode of decorative design'.[16] Wollaton and Hardwick are, in both plan-outline and elevation, strongly symmetrical and display classical elements in their details, but they are far from classical in the generally accepted definition. But architecture has other concerns than style. In other studies, I have pointed to the manner in which the designs of Palladio and Smythson evince a deep response to the physical climates within which they are set.[17] In Palladio's case, the question of climate is made explicit in *I Quattro Libri*, where he gives precise prescriptions on how to determine the sizes of windows in relation to the climate of the Veneto and is similarly precise in discussing the design of fireplaces and chimneys.[18] The question is whether such a relationship between theory and practice, or science and craft, existed in England. Can Smythson's designs be regarded as *scientific*?

The plans of Wollaton and Hardwick are similar in their bi-axial symmetries. At Wollaton, the almost square plan is elaborated with four corner turrets. Hardwick is rectangular, with turrets in two groups of three at either end (Figure 6.3). Each house has a dramatic silhouette that is further emphasised by their hilltop locations. In the sixteenth century, northern Europe was in the depths of the so-called 'Little Ice Age'.[19] In the British climate,

Figure 6.2 Robert Smythson, Hardwick Hall, from west. (Dean Hawkes)

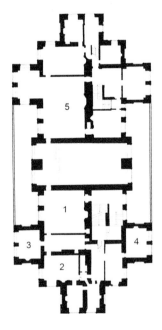

Figure 6.3 Hardwick Hall, First Floor Plan. (Dean Hawkes)

at latitudes spanning between 50° and 58° N, the orientation of a building has a great effect on the conditions within. Wollaton is oriented with the cardinals almost precisely on the diagonal of the plan, and, at Hardwick, the long axis of the plan lies a fraction from due north–south. These facts allow us to analyse the environmental sophistication of the buildings.

Wollaton is entered from the northwest, and a complex, sheltering, draught-excluding route leads to the central Hall. This is lit by high clerestory windows on all four sides and is warmed by two great fireplaces. The central location insulates the space against the cold. Two of the most important rooms in the house are the Dining Room on the ground floor and the South Great Chamber immediately above it on the first floor. The Dining Room was probably the most densely inhabited room in the house. This is where the women of the household spent most of their time in the winter months and where the entire household would dine.[20] The room has a large fireplace on the inner wall. The South Great Chamber was the principal ceremonial room and is matched by a similar space on the north side of the plan. The inventory of the contents of the house, made in 1601, refers to 'the southe great chamber alias the best chamber' and lists its lavish furnishings in contrast to the sparse contents of the north chamber.[21] The windows in the south-facing chamber have larger areas of glazing than their counterparts to the north, in further acknowledgement of the distinction between the different aspects.

Hardwick Hall was built for Elizabeth, Countess of Shrewsbury, who was 70 years old when the house was completed in 1597.[22] The twentieth-century English architect, Peter Smithson, was a great admirer of the house. He wrote:

> In Hardwick Hall there is a gallery that runs along the whole extent of the house. What's nice about (the plan) is that it indicates the thick spine wall, where the fireplaces are ... and the perimeter windows that let the light in.[23]

This description refers to the second floor of the house, the site of the great ceremonial rooms, where the relationship between the masonry spine wall and the glassy perimeter is most clearly seen. Throughout the house the tall windows fill the interior with natural light, a necessity in a period when artificial light sources were minimal in quality and number. The inventory of the contents of the house made in 1601, just four years after its completion, tells us that there were two hanging candelabras in the double-height Great Hall on the ground floor, plus four candlesticks fixed to the walls.[24] Other than these, the inventory lists just 25 candlesticks that would be carried around the house to light the way and illuminate rooms as they were occupied. It has been observed that at this date, Shakespeare's day, the difference between day and night was extreme, particularly in the winter months. 'In the age of candle and rush-light, nights were seriously dark'.[25] The house was heated by 31 fireplaces, fuelled by wood from the woods and copses on the estate and, in some cases, by coal from the estate's own mines. These fireplaces, in the thick masonry walls at the centre of the house, warmed the great mass of the building and offered some compensation for the inevitable cold of the glassy perimeter.

The strict symmetry of the exterior conceals a remarkable freedom in the internal organisation of the house. My analysis proposes that this is a specific response to questions of comfort in the harsh climate of the time. It is no accident that the principal apartments are all placed at the southern end of the plan. There they benefit from the warmth of the sun as it tracks from east to west. The ground floor houses the chambers for senior members of the household, including a nursery for the countess' grandchildren. Immediately above these are the countess' own apartments, a Withdrawing Chamber and bedroom and a bedroom for her older granddaughter. Here, protected by floors below and above, these relatively small rooms receive the best of the sun, and their open fires easily warm them.[26] On the top floor, the High Great Chamber occupies the entire south-west corner. This is the principal room of the house and the site of great feasts and events. At this time of night-time darkness, dinner and other ceremonials began in mid-afternoon, to enjoy the daylight that flooded into the room.

It is clear that these buildings, in their form, planning and materiality, represent a deep understanding of the climate of England. The question is whether this understanding may be regarded as *scientific*. As we saw earlier, architecture had a place in the taxonomy of sixteenth-century science, as one of the *Mechanical Arts*. To what extent did this status bear upon the conscious practises of a man such as Robert Smythson? Girouard suggests that Smythson's designs are fundamentally a continuation of the native Gothic vernacular tradition and, thus, implicitly lie outside the realm of science.[27] But, in my analysis of their response to the English climate, buildings such as Wollaton and Hardwick mark a radical step away from the procedures of the vernacular. At a time when our modern concepts of climate and comfort were unrecognised and lay beyond numerical description, it may be suggested that Smythson achieved a sophistication and consistency, precision without number, that places them firmly within the realm of the science of their time.[28]

Architecture and science in the seventeenth century

Christopher Wren (1632–1723) was first a scientist and then an architect, so his education and practice backgrounds were quite unlike those of Robert Smythson. John Summerson has explored the broad relationship between Wren's science and his architecture. In setting the scene on this relationship in the seventeenth century, Summerson wrote,

> For us today the problem is bedevilled by those distinctions between 'scientific' and 'artistic' which were erected during the course of the nineteenth century and which it is exceedingly misleading to apply to

the seventeenth. It is equally bedevilled by the element of rationalism which has crept into our notion of architecture, so that the idea of a 'scientist' becoming an 'architect' immediately suggests the application of some special rigour of a 'functional' kind to design problems.[29]

Wren's Sheldonian Theatre at Oxford plays a key part in Summerson's analysis (Figure 6.4). On 29 April 1663, Wren exhibited a model of the building at a meeting of the Royal Society; an event that, perhaps, suggests the unity of the 'scientific' and the 'artistic'. At the end of the same year, on 9 December, Wren presented a design for a 'weather-clock' to the Society. This clockwork device plotted recordings of air temperature, barometric pressure and wind speed and direction (Figure 6.5).[30] The instrument was inspired by a never realised project to construct 'A History of the Seasons'.[31] Summerson suggests that the 'immature' architecture of the Sheldonian is reminiscent of the 'decorative trimmings' of the weather-clock.[32] He contrasts the 'artistic' shortcomings of the visible architecture, exterior and interior, with the sophistication of the 'scientific' design of the concealed roof trusses that span the wide space below – 'a real piece of Royal Society research'. But he also insists that the designing of a classical façade and a

Figure 6.4 Christopher Wren, Sheldonian Theatre, Oxford, south front. (Dean Hawkes)

Figure 6.5 Christopher Wren, Weather Clock. (The Royal Society)

new kind of roof truss were not, for Wren and his contemporaries, in any way in conflict, 'The fact is that to them the natural equivalent of scientific thought in architecture was classical design'.

In research published in 2012, the author examined a number of Wren's buildings from an environmental perspective and suggested that they demonstrate a previously unidentified connection between his scientific knowledge and his architecture.[33] The Sheldonian Theatre is an ideal example. The building was designed primarily to accommodate the annual university degree ceremony, the Encaenia, which is held on the Wednesday of the ninth week of the university's Trinity Term. This is the week of the summer solstice. In addition, the building was used for musical performances and as an anatomy theatre. It was also the home of the university printing press. Nonetheless, the Encaenia was its principal raison d'etre and it was this that most fundamentally influenced the design. The plan is usually said to derive from the Theatre of Marcellus, as illustrated by Vitruvius and Serlio. But a roofed space in seventeenth-century England is very different from an open-air theatre in Roman Italy.

The Encaenia is a day-long ceremony that takes place before a large audience, all in heavy academical dress. In the week of the summer solstice, the interior would have ample daylight throughout the day, but the crowded room would be in danger of becoming very hot. These conditions are directly addressed in the design. The building stands to the north of the Duke Humfrey's building of the Bodleian Library, built in 1488, and is entered from the south through the classical façade. The amphitheatre is illuminated by great windows, ranging in orientation from east, through north, to west, above and below the gallery. Twentieth-century building science tells us that under the usually dull, but changeable English sky, good light in a building depends on providing an unobstructed view of a good portion of the sky; the 'sky component' of the 'daylight factor'.[34] This is precisely what Wren's fenestration provides. By virtue of the orientation of the building, it also limits the amount of direct sunlight that will enter during the long summer day. In addition, the arrangement provided effective and necessary cross-ventilation. A contemporary description is given in Robert Plot's *The Natural History of Oxfordshire*, published in 1677.[35] In this he gives a detailed account of the ingenuity of the design of the windows and their opening mechanisms that provide copious ventilation, but prevent the ingress of rain, an important matter in the English climate. Alongside *light* and *heat*, the third element of the scientific architectural environment is *sound*, its acoustics. These were admired at the opening of the building on 19 July 1669, and celebrated in a Pindaric Ode, *In Theatrum Sheldonianum et eius Architectum*, that was delivered on the day. This reports that there were no unwanted echoes and that both words and music were heard with 'pleasing purity'.[36] Was this coincidence, or is it further evidence of Wren's 'scientific' understanding brought to bear on this often-problematic aspect of design?

Notwithstanding his critique of the artistic merit of the Sheldonian Theatre, Summerson was fulsome in his recognition of the building's place in the unfolding story of the relation of architecture and science in England:

> of all buildings (the Sheldonian) most exactly reflects the early image of (the Royal Society) and embodies its philosophy.
>
> the Theatre is the dispensation of a mode of thought most obviously manifested in the field which we now call science, but which can be seen more rarely to have left its imprint on the arts and especially in architecture.
>
> everything in this building wears the livery of the Experimental Philosophy and of the Society with whose founding members it was so concerned.
>
> It reflects, like no other I can think of, a crucial phase in our intellectual history – a phase of energy and optimism when the arts and sciences were conceived to be as symmetrically and devotedly disposed about Truth.[37]

The greatest architectural project of Wren's life, with the exception of the building of St. Paul's cathedral, was the rebuilding of London's churches following the destruction caused by the Great Fire of 1666.[38] In 1670, the Rebuilding Act set up commissioners to direct the reconstruction of churches, and Parliament authorised a list of no less than 51 buildings. This began a process that involved Wren for the next 40 years. In 1708, an act of Parliament recommended the construction of a further 50 churches in the city, and Wren, then 76 years old, took the opportunity to set out clear principles to guide the design of these.[39] The 'Letter to a Friend on the Commission for Building Fifty New Churches' contains a set of objective prescriptions on the practical aspects of designing churches for 'the new reformed religion', that of post-Restoration Anglicanism. In my analysis I propose that these are a demonstration of Wren's *scientific* approach to questions of light and sound in this new configuration of space for worship. He proposed that churches should be designed for a congregation of two thousand in which,

> All who are present can both hear and see. The Romanists indeed, may build larger churches, it is enough if they hear the Murmur of the Mass, and see the Elevation of the Host, but ours are to be fitted as Auditories.

The concern for daylight and acoustics brings exactly the same priorities to the design of sacred space as Wren applied to the Sheldonian Theatre. Beginning with acoustics, he offered a mathematical formula, 'Concerning the Placement of the Pulpit',

> 'A moderate voice may be heard 50 feet distant before the preacher, 30 feet on each side and 20 behind the pulpit.'

From this, Wren calculated that a church 'should be at least 60 Feet broad and 90 Feet long'. The entire topography of the building follows from this, as sound lines and sight lines are precisely organised. The clearest demonstration of this is St James's Church, Piccadilly (1676–1684) (Figure 6.6), which Wren specifically refers to in the 'Letter'. This was not one of the post-Fire reconstructions, standing as it does outside the bounds of the City of London, but was, for Wren, a clear exemplar of his principles. The plan is a simple rectangle with galleried aisles on either side of a barrel-vaulted nave. This brings the entire congregation within good hearing distance of the pulpit, which is placed at the south side of the chancel. The arrangement also provides good sight lines. The same process that was successful at the Sheldonian Theatre works here to address the difficulties of daylighting under English skies. Tall windows above the galleries fill the space with light from north and south, with smaller lights below to illuminate the aisles. From all points of the interior, there is a clear view of the sky above the surrounding buildings; once again, in modern terminology, achieving a high sky component of the daylight factor.[40]

As Summerson reminds us, Wren would not recognise the modern distinction between *scientific* and *artistic* modes of thought and action.[41] Nonetheless his designs for the Sheldonian Theatre and the city churches

Figure 6.6 Christopher Wren, St. James's, Piccadilly, Interior. (Dean Hawkes)

mark a fundamental shift of method when compared with that of Robert Smythson, less than a century before. This is not a question of stylistic change – although Wren's buildings are clearly 'classical', whilst Smythson's are not. What is identifiable in these later buildings is their direct response to the specific requirements of their use: university ceremonies or a new conception of religious space, respectively. Before the availability of effective sources of artificial light, daylight was the only means of achieving high levels of illumination in buildings. Wren's designs achieve this by placing and sizing windows to maximise the view of unobstructed sky within, in arrangements that respect the formal rules of classical composition, what Summerson described as, 'the natural equivalent of scientific thought'. Clear glass and light-coloured interior finishes reinforce the geometry of these. On acoustics, the prescription for hearing in the city churches could equally apply to the satisfactory sound within the Sheldonian.

We have no documentary evidence that Wren applied *scientific* procedures in designing the environments in these buildings, but his 'weather-clocks' and other experiments with meteorological instruments tell us that he has a direct, quantitative interest in meteorology, which could inform judgements about buildings. Similarly, an astronomer's understanding of the earth's movement in relation to the sun – the passage of the days and seasons – would bring precision to an architect's ability to achieve both 'practical' and 'artistic' illumination in spaces. This is amply shown in the diversity of lights found in the city churches.[42] In little over half a century after the completion of Robert Smythson's last buildings, architecture in England had changed almost beyond recognition, and we may suggest that in Wren's work, the art of architecture had found common ground with the emerging organised science represented by the Royal Society of which he was a founding member and an active participant for the remainder of his long life.

Architecture and science in the eighteenth century

Summerson tells us that English architecture in the first half of the eighteenth century was the product of the 'Rule of Taste'.[43] The familiar label for this architecture is 'Palladian', and Summerson locates its origins in the publication of two books, Colen Campbell's *Vitruvius Britannicus*[44] and the first English translation, by Giacomo Leoni, of Andrea Palladio's, *I Quattro Libri dell'Architettura*.[45] Campbell's book is a collection of engravings of English country houses by architects including Wren, Thomas Archer, Inigo Jones and Campbell himself. The text is almost entirely descriptive, giving dimensions of the buildings, discussing the materials used and aspects of the classical style. In contrast, Palladio's celebrated text is a comprehensive manual on almost all aspects of architecture. It is, of course, an architecture that is precisely located in the conditions – cultural and geographical – of Italy. On the environmental matters that are our concern here, the prescriptions for the orientation of rooms, the dimensioning of windows or the size and location of fireplaces are all calibrated to the Italian climate and, specifically, that of the Veneto.

The English Palladians were, from the outset, alert to the different conditions of the English climate to which they quite precisely adapted their designs. In the first volume of *Vitruvius Britannicus*, Campbell illustrated his design for Wanstead House (1715–1720). From this we may obtain an idea of this process of climate adaptation by noting the larger dimensions of the windows in relation to room sizes, compared to the Italian precedents. This provides more daylight under the duller English skies, whilst not suffering the overheating that would be experienced from the Italian sun. Palladio recommended that fireplaces should be placed on the outside walls of rooms, but at Wanstead they are on the internal walls, in the traditional English manner that allows the heat to be retained in the core of the building during the colder winters.

A significant moment in the translation of Palladian principles to the English context came with the writings of Robert Morris (1703–1754). Describing himself as a 'Surveyor', Morris published a number of works on architecture in the first half of the eighteenth century.[46] Of particular relevance here are the *Lectures on Architecture* (1734–36). Broadly conforming to the model of

Palladio's treatise, the lectures comprised a broad historical review, a discourse on proportion and illustrations of unbuilt designs by the author. But it is their relation to the new scientific culture in eighteenth-century England that is most relevant here. Tanis Hinchcliffe has argued that the *Lectures* were conceived in 'a language close to the Newtonian tradition of scientific lectures and publishing'.[47] A key element of that tradition was the application of rational principles to actions in the natural world. Hinchcliffe writes,

> For Morris, architecture existed in the physical world, where there is natural and artificial architecture, but the physical world should be experienced through experiment, not simply through custom. Just as he would have encountered experiments in public display of science, so Morris recommends that building technology be handled experimentally on a day-to-day basis by those engaged in the process.[48]

In translating 'rational principles' into practical guidance for architecture, Morris adopted the Newtonian practice of quantification and tabulation. In Lecture II, the influence of Newton is apparent when introducing the subject of lighting rooms:

> OPTICKS will be requisite to be understood, as far as they relate to Proportions of Light in large or small Rooms, or as the Situation is as to the four Cardinal Points.

In Lecture VII, a procedure is given for determining the dimensions of windows:

> By which any room may be illuminated more or less according to the Uses of them ...
>   Let the Magnitude of the Room be given, and one of those Proportions I have propos'd to be made use of, or any other; multiply the Length and Breadth of the Room together, and that Product multiply by the Height, and the Square Root of that Sum will be the area or superficial Content in Feet, etc. of Light requir'd.[49]

This clearly derives from Palladio's method in Chapter XXV of the First Book but is more explicit in its formulation by giving 'worked examples' for various types and sizes of rooms. It also differs in that the resultant windows are consistently larger in relation to the rooms they serve than the Italian examples, making them suitable to the duller light of England.

Lecture VI is concerned with the 'Situation' of houses, and it is here that the relevance of reference to the Cardinal Points becomes apparent:

> The South Aspect is most preferable for the principal Front, if it can be conveniently had, in which should be the Rooms of State and Grandeur.

> The East is most proper for a library, because in the Morning Sun gives an enlivening Warmth to nature.[50]

This Lecture concludes with a discourse on the calculation of sizes of chimneys in relation to the dimensions of rooms. The formula is summarised in 'A Table of Harmonick and Arithmetical Proportions for Magnitudes of Rooms and Chimnies by Universal Rules'.

A quarter of a century after Morris delivered his lectures, William Chambers (1723–1796) published *A Treatise on the Decorative Part of Civil Architecture*.[51] This also follows the model of Palladio but is more explicit than Morris in its translation of the specific details of design for the English condition.

> In Italy, and some other hot countries, although the windows are less in general than ours, their apartments cannot be made habitable, but by keeping the window shutters almost closed, while the sun appears above the horizon. But in regions where gloom and clouds prevail eight months of the year, it will always be right a sufficiency of light for those melancholy seasons.

In the new *scientific* spirit, Chambers declares Palladio's formula for window size to be 'surely too vague' and, on the authority of his own practice, proposes an alternative:

> I have generally added the depth and the height of the rooms on the principal floor together, and taken one eighth-part thereof, for the width of the window; a rule to which there are few objections; admitting somewhat more light than Palladio's, it is, I apprehend, fitter for our climate than his rule would be.

Chambers also confirms that Palladio's practice of placing fireplaces on the outer wall of a building was unsuitable in England. '(T)his must be avoided for ... the chimney shafts at the top of the building, which must necessarily be carried higher than the ridges of the roofs, have from their great length, a very disagreeable effect'. A simple formula is then given by which to calculate the size of a fireplace in relation to the dimensions of a room.

Theory and practice enjoy a curious relationship in the architecture of eighteenth-century England. It is clear that the publication of Campbell's *Vitruvius Britannicus* and Leoni's English translation of Palladio had a profound, formative effect on practice, but it is an intriguing fact that the precise adjustments of the Italian precedents, in both theory and practice, were anticipated in the first great English Palladian houses, all of which predate the writings of Morris and Chambers. Wanstead (1715–1720) was demolished in 1820, but Houghton Hall (1722–1725), Mereworth Castle (1723) and Chiswick House (1725–1729) (Figure 6.7) have all survived and display windows larger than

Figure 6.7 Lord Burlington, Chiswick House, entrance front. (Dean Hawkes)

those found in the Veneto. Similarly, the provision of fireplaces and chimneys is generous in number and dimension and almost always these are located on the inner walls, as may be seen in the plan of Houghton. The exception to this 'rule' is at Chiswick where the fireplaces are, as in the model at Palladio's Rotonda, on the outer walls, although the obelisk-like chimneys rise higher above the eaves than those at Vicenza, as was later stipulated by Chambers.

Summerson suggests that, in adopting the Palladian 'style', the English architects of the eighteenth century were seeking to make a clean break from the earlier tradition of classical architecture in the country, 'the works of Sir Christopher Wren in particular and anything in the nature of Baroque'.[52] On the other hand, it may be argued that the 'new' architecture embraced a 'scientific cast of mind'[53] that, although influenced by Newtonian codification and tabulation, may be traced back to the scientific thought that was developed by Christopher Wren in the previous century and, perhaps, even to the architecture of precision without number that may be found in the works of Robert Smythson.

Conclusion

This essay has sought to uncover the way in which architecture and science in England were interrelated in the two hundred years between the last decades of the sixteenth century and the middle years of the eighteenth. Through a study of the remarkable houses by Robert Smythson, we may see that the relationship between building and climate – the extreme climate of the 'Little Ice Age' – achieved a consistency and precision of design that moves beyond the conventions and practices of vernacular precedent. In this sense they are becoming *scientific*. Christopher Wren was a scientist who became an architect. This link has been discussed previously in broad critical terms,[54] but the present study shows that Wren's work in the field of meteorology, in tandem with the implications of his understanding of astronomy in considering the natural lighting of buildings, makes him possibly the first *building scientist*. In the eighteenth century, the architecture of the English Palladians became allied with the 'scientific cast of mind' that spread through the culture under the influence of Newton. The treatises of Morris and Chambers adopted Newtonian codification and tabulation in recalibrating the Italian architecture of Palladio to the different conditions of England, thus combining architectural style with the numerical systems of science.

The conventional reading of the relationship between architecture and science rests upon the link between science and technology that emerged at the end of the eighteenth century, as new methods of construction and environmental provision were taken into building practice. By the twentieth century, for some, architecture and technology had become almost inseparable. As Gropius argued, 'A breach has been made with the past, which allows us to envisage a new aspect of architecture corresponding to the technical civilisation of the age we live in'.[55] In twenty-first-century theory and practice, it is almost inconceivable that a building would not involve some measure of numerical calculation in the design of its structure, fabric and, in relation to the present discussion, its environmental services. To paraphrase Siegfried Giedion, 'mechanisation *has taken* command'. This essay argues that science in architecture has a validity and relevance that is independent of this conventional, instrumental relationship between science and technology. The early modern buildings of Smythson, Wren and the English Palladians were conceived within an evolving conception of science that carries implications for our present understanding of this complex relationship. They show us that a scientific grasp of the natural world may be seamlessly incorporated into the processes by which works of architecture are conceived, that a building may be *scientific* without recourse to the literal translation of its science into overt technological expression.

Notes

1 This essay was first published in *Wolkencuckucksheim*, Volume 19, No. 33, 2014, pp. 47–62.
2 Important texts of particular relevance to the relation of technology and architecture are: Sigfried Giedion, *Mechanization Takes Command: A Contribution to Anonymous History*, Oxford, Oxford University Press, 1948, and Lewis Mumford, *Technics and Civilization*, London, Routledge, 1934. Reyner

Banham's *The Architecture of the Well-Tempered Environment*, London, The Architectural Press, 1969, opened up the study of environmental science and technology that has been developed further by the present author and others. See Dean Hawkes, *The Environmental Tradition*, London & New York, E & FN Spon, 1996, *The Environmental Imagination*, London & New York, Routledge, 2008, 2nd Edition, 2020 and *Architecture and Climate*, London & New York, Routledge, 2012.

3 Joseph Gwilt, *An Encyclopaedia of Architecture: Historical, Theoretical and Practical*, London, Longmans, Brown & Green, 1st Edition, 1825. Further editions, 1836, 1867, 1876 and 1888. The book remained in print into the twentieth century.

4 See F.M. Lea, *History of the Building Research Station*, London, HMSO, 1974, and Sigurd Fleckner, *Reichsforschungsgesellschaft für Wirtschaftlichkeit in Bau und Wohnungswesen*, Aachen, RWTH Publications, 1993.

5 Modern working definitions of these terms are: *Science*, noun: the intellectual and practical activity encompassing the systematic study of the structure and behaviour of the physical and natural world through observation and experiment. *Technology*, noun: the application of scientific knowledge for practical purposes. *Oxford English Dictionary*, 2001 Edition.

6 Katherine Park and Lorraine Daston (Eds.), *The Cambridge History of Science, Volume 3, Early Modern Science*, Cambridge, Cambridge University Press, 2006.

7 Ibid.

8 James Bennett, 'The Mechanical Arts', in Park and Daston (Eds.), op cit.

9 W.E. Knowles Middleton, *Invention of the Meteorological Instruments*, Baltimore, MD, The Johns Hopkins Press, 1969.

10 Adrian Johns, 'Coffee Houses and Print Shops', in Park and Daston (Eds.), op cit.

11 Mark Girouard, *Robert Smythson and the English Country House*, New Haven, CT, & London, Yale University Press, 1983.

12 John Summerson, *Architecture in Britain 1530–1830*, Harmondsworth, Penguin Books, 1969.

13 Mark Girouard, 1983, op cit.

14 Mark Girouard, 'The Smythson Collection of the Royal Institute of British Architects', *Architectural History*, Vol. 5, 1962, pp. 21–184.

15 Summerson, 1969, op cit.

16 Ibid.

17 Dean Hawkes, *The Environmental Tradition: Studies in the Architecture of Environment*, London & New York, E & FN Spon, 1996.

18 Andrea Palladio, *I Quattro Libri dell'Architettura*, Venice, 1570, English translation, Isaac Ware, London, 1738; facsimile edition, New York, Dover Publications Inc., 1965.

19 Brian Fagan, *The Little Ice Age: How Climate made History*, New York, Basic Books, 2002.

20 See, Pamela Marshall, *Wollaton Hall: An Archaeological Survey*, Nottingham, Nottingham Civic Society, 1996, and Alice T. Friedman, *House and Household in Elizabethan England: Wollaton Hall and the Willoughby Family*, Chicago, IL, University of Chicago Press, 1989.

21 Inventory presented in Pamela Marshall, *Wollaton Hall: An Archaeological Survey*, op cit.

22 The environment of Hardwick is discussed in detail in Essay Six, 'The Environment of the Elizabethan house: Hardwick Hall'.

23 Peter Smithson, *Conversations with Students: A Space for Our Generation*, Princeton, NJ, Princeton University Press, 2005.

24 Lindsay Boynton (Ed.), *The Hardwick Hall Inventory of 1601*, London, The Furniture History Society, 1971.
25 Jonathan Bate, 'Introduction to 'A Midsummer Night's Dream', in Jonathan Bate and Eric Rasmussen (Eds.), *William Shakespeare: Complete Works*, London, The Royal Shakespeare Company/Macmillan, 2007.
26 The furnishings of these rooms included warm carpets, thick curtains and coverlets. All to complement and retain the warmth of the open fires. See, *The Hardwick Hall Inventory of 1601*, op cit.
27 Girouard, 1983, op cit.
28 See the following for recent, detailed studies of the environment of Hardwick Hall. Ranald Lawrence and Dean Hawkes, 'Describing the Historic Indoor Climate: Thermal Monitoring at Hardwick Hall', *Architectural Science Review*, 2020, pp. 293–316. Dean Hawkes and Ranald Lawrence, 'Climate, Comfort and Architecture in Elizabethan England: An Environmental Study of Hardwick Hall', *The Journal of Architecture*, Vol. 26, Issue 4, online, 2021. 32pp.
29 See, John Summerson, 'The Mind of Wren', in John Summerson, *Heavenly Mansions and Other Essays on Architecture*, London, Cresset Press, 1949. A later essay is, 'Christopher Wren: Why Architecture?', in John Summerson, *The Unromantic Castle and Other Essays*, London & New York, Thames & Hudson, 1990. A study specifically concerned with the link between architecture and science in Wren is, J.A. Bennett, *The Mathematical Sciences of Christopher Wren*, Cambridge, Cambridge University Press, 1982.
30 See J.A. Bennett, 1982, op cit, and A.J. Biswas, 'The Automatic Rain-Gauge of Sir Christopher Wren FRS', *Notes and Records of the Royal Society*, Vol. 22, 1967, pp. 94–104.
31 The proposal is outlined in Christopher Wren, Junior, *Parentalia*, the collection of family documents compiled by Wren's son and published in 1750. Reprinted edition, London, The Gregg Press, 1965.
32 John Summerson, 1990, op cit.
33 Dean Hawkes, 'Christopher Wren and the Origins of Building Science', in *Architecture and Climate*, 2012, op cit.
34 See, R.G. Hopkinson, *Architectural Physics: Lighting*, London, HMSO, 1963.
35 Robert Plot, *The Natural History of Oxfordshire*, Oxford, printed at the Theatre, 1667.
36 Lisa Jardine, *On a Grander Scale: The Outstanding Career of Christopher Wren*, London, Harper Collins, 2002.
37 John Summerson, *The Sheldonian in Its Time*, Oxford, The Clarendon Press, 1964.
38 Paul Jeffrey, *The City Churches of Sir Christopher Wren*, London, Hambledon Continuum, 1996.
39 'Letter to a Friend on the Commission for Building Fifty New Churches', in Christopher Wren Junior, *Parentalia*, op cit. The 'Letter' is reproduced in full in Lydia Soo, *Wren's Tracts on Architecture and Other Writing*, Cambridge, Cambridge University Press, 1998.
40 In seventeenth-century London most of the surrounding buildings were lower than their modern replacements, but St. James's remains the 'lightbox' that Wren intended.
41 John Summerson, 1990, op cit.
42 Dean Hawkes, 'Christopher Wren and the Origins of Building Science', in *Architecture and Climate*, op cit.
43 John Summerson, 1969, op cit.
44 Colen Campbell, *Vitruvius Britannicus*, London, Vols. I–III, 1715, 1717, 1725, Facsimilie edition Vols. 1–3, New York, Dover Publications, 2007.

45 Andrea Palladio, *Il quattro libri dell'architettura*, op cit.
46 Robert Morris, *An Essay in Defence of Ancient Architecture*, London, 1728; *Lectures on Architecture* (2 Vols,), London, J. Brindley, 1734–1736; *Rural Architecture*, London, 1750; *Architectural Remembrancer*, London, 1751.
47 Tanis Hinchcliffe, 'Robert Morris: Architecture and the Scientific Cast of Mind', *Architectural History*, Vol. 47, 2004, pp. 127–138.
48 Ibid.
49 Robert Morris, *Lectures on Architecture*, op cit.
50 Ibid.
51 William Chambers, *A Treatise on the Decorative Part of Civil Architecture*, London, 1759. Facsimilie edition, New York, Dover Publications, 2001.
52 John Summerson, 1969, op cit.
53 Tanis Hinchcliffe, 2004, op cit.
54 John Summerson, 1949, op cit and J.A. Bennett, 1982, op cit.
55 Walter Gropius, *The New Architecture and the Bauhaus*, London, Faber & Faber, 1935.

Essay 7[1]
The measurable and the unmeasurable of daylight design

> Architecture comes from the making of a room. A room is not a room without natural light.
>
> *– Louis Kahn, 1971*[2]

Introduction

In his deceptively simple statement, inscribed on a beautiful drawing (Figure 7.1), Louis Kahn lays down a profound challenge. The implication is that light in architecture is needed not only to serve practical purposes but is the key to the definition of architecture itself.

One of the most important achievements of nineteenth- and twentieth-century applied science has been to quantify and codify human requirements in buildings. This has been particularly successful in lighting design, where standards of illumination, design procedures and rules-of-thumb are to be found in many design manuals and guidebooks. Familiar rules-of-thumb include geometrical formulae such as the 'no-sky line', where the depth of penetration of the visible sky is taken to indicate the limit of the daylit area of a sidelit room. Others are expressed in simple equations in which the daylight factor of a room is related to the ratio of window area to floor area. These tools are of immense utility and place practical design on solid foundations. In recent years, they have been complemented by the development of computer-based calculation methods and simulation tools.

But there is much more to daylighting design than this and, once again, it is Louis Kahn who gets to the nub of the matter.

> I only wish that the first really worthwhile discovery of science would be that it recognised that the unmeasureable is what they're really fighting to understand, and that the measureable is only the servant of the unmeasureable; that everything that man makes must be fundamentally unmeasureable.[3]

DOI: 10.4324/9781003083023-8

The plan. A society of rooms is a place good to learn, work, live.

Architecture comes from The Making of a Room

A great American Poet once asked The Architect 'What slice of the sun does your building have. What light enters your Room as if to say the sun never knew how great it is until it struck the side of a building.

The Room

is The place of the mind. In a small room one does not say what one would in a large room. In a room with only one other person could be generative. The vectors of each meet. natural light gives the time of day and the moon of the seasons to enter. A room is not a room without natural light.

Figure 7.1 Louis Kahn, 'Architecture comes from the making of a room'. (Philadelphia Museum of Art © Estate of Louis I. Kahn)

Here Kahn presents a conundrum. What is the value of quantification and codification, the measureable, if we are really trying to understand the essence of architecture, the unmeasurable? How may we solve the puzzle?

It is a truism that architecture is a combination of art and science. This is clearly reflected in the conventional categories of architectural literature and in the curricula of schools of architecture, where all too often the two realms remain firmly separate. But this does not help us solve Kahn's conundrum, so where do we look?

My suggestion is that, whilst aspects of art and science certainly pertain to questions of architecture, it is not possible to construct a proper understanding of its true nature by applying a simplistic equation of the form – *art* + *science* = *architecture*. In the search for an answer, we should turn to the evidence of buildings themselves, of works of architecture, and to the statements of architects of substance, which, if correctly interpreted, provide deep insights into the matter. I propose a mode of architectural analysis and interpretation that allows us to look directly into Kahn's architectural 'unmeasurable'.

In *The Environmental Imagination*,[4] I made a series of studies of works by architects that spanned the nineteenth and twentieth centuries, precisely paralleling the period when the modern quantification of environmental design took place. In more recent work, *Architecture and Climate*,[5] I have pushed back the historical time frame to explore works from the sixteenth to the eighteenth centuries. In this I have argued that the crucial instrument of understanding, of looking into the unmeasurable, has been the imagination, defined by my dictionary as, 'the faculty of forming new ideas'. To illustrate my meaning, I will consider a sequence of buildings from the seventeenth to the twenty-first centuries that illustrate the effectiveness of imagination in the conception of daylight.

Christopher Wren: geometry and light

The first case is from the works of Sir Christopher Wren. He was both scientist and architect and, before his first works as an architect, he held professorships of astronomy, first in London and then in Oxford. One of Wren's greatest architectural achievements was the reconstruction of over fifty London churches, following the devastation of the Great Fire of 1666. One of the most significant of these is the church of St. Stephen Walbrook (1672–1680).[6] Here an apparently simple rectangular plan develops into a cross-section that plays upon the juxtaposition of a nave with aisles and a centralised plan, surmounted by a dome. This produces great complexity of space and light. The light from large windows in the enclosing walls is supplemented by arched clerestories orientated to the four points of the compass, north, south, east and west, and by the lantern at the apex of the dome. Wren was fastidious in attending to the practical illumination of the space, but his intentions extended beyond the merely practical. As the historian Kerry Downes has written of St. Stephen:

> Wren considered geometry to be the basis of the whole world and the manifestation of its Creator, while light not only made that geometry visible, but also represented the gift of Reason, of which geometry was for him the highest expression.[7]

In the interior of St. Stephen (Figure 7.2), the alternating patterns of light and shade, the sudden and brief illumination of the shaft of a column, that reshape the space from hour to hour and from season to season, reveal how Wren's scientific understanding of light was transformed by his remarkable architectural imagination.

Soane and Scarpa: poets of daylight

Another English architect whose work exhibits an imagination equal to that of Wren is Sir John Soane. He worked at precisely the time when the industrial revolution was transforming the technologies of building and was a leading exponent in the application of these to architecture, but he, like

Figure 7.2 Christopher Wren, St Stephen Walbrook Church, interior. (Dean Hawkes)

Wren, was simultaneously engaged with exploring the qualitative, poetic aspects of light in architecture:

> The 'lumière mystérieuse' so successfully practised by the French artists, is a most powerful agent in the hands of a man of genius, and its power cannot be too fully understood, nor too highly appreciated. It is, however, little attended to in our architecture, and for this obvious reason, that we do not sufficiently feel the importance of character in our buildings, to which the mode of admitting light contributes in no small degree.[8]

In the design of his house at 12–14 Lincoln's Inn Fields in the centre of London, which he occupied and transformed in the years from 1792 until his death in 1837, Soane seized the opportunity to explore the character of natural light to sustain both the practical and poetic needs of the act of dwelling.[9] These were met by the richest and most diverse architectural means, adopting both side lighting and rooflights in a variety of combinations to light spaces of immense richness. The library and drawing room are interconnected spaces at the ground floor of the main body of the house. The library lies behind the principal, south-facing façade and the dining room is lit from an open courtyard to the north. The walls of both rooms are a deep Pompeian red. This absorbs much of the

Figure 7.3 John Soane, House at 12–14 Lincoln's Inn Fields, London, breakfast
room. (Edwin Smith/RIBA Collections)

light that enters, but ample compensation comes from the arrays of large and
small mirrors that supplement and transform both the quantity and quality of
the light. Some of the most effective of these are those that line the piers of the
glazed loggia to the south and the sliding shutters at the windows. The breakfast room is one of Soane's most remarkable inventions and, as always, the
preoccupation is with light. (Figure 7.3) This compressed, land-locked space
is lit by the ingenious combination of a small lantern placed in the canopy of
the vaulted ceiling, directly above the breakfast table, and two linear lights,
glazed with yellow-tinted glass, that wash the yellow painted north and south
walls. The effect of these is softened by the sidelight that enters through the
window that overlooks the adjacent Monument Yard, the east light of morning appropriately illuminating breakfast. By these, and numerous other similar
devices, the rooms are simultaneously sombre and sparkling, lumière mysté-
rieuse brought to the service of domestic life and of architecture.

Moving to examples from the twentieth century. Boris Podrecca has
written:

> In (Carlo) Scarpa's work it is not just the physical presence of things
> that transfigures tradition, but also the light, which is a lumen not of

tomorrow but of the past – the light of the golden background, of the glimmering liquid, of the ivory-coloured inlay, of luminous and shimmering fabrics recreated in marble. It is the light of a reflection of the world.[10]

These qualities are fully demonstrated in the tiny addition that Scarpa built to the Museo Canoviano at Possagno in the 1950s.[11] The composition pivots around a tall, cubic space, lit by four trihedral corner windows high in the walls (Figure 7.4). Two of these face west and are tall and concave, the others are to the east and the glass enclosure is convex. The view from within is solely of the sky. This configuration captures light from all orientations and, unlike a conventional window set in a wall, casts light across the walls themselves in addition to directing it into the space. As the sun moves around the building, the interior and Canova's precious and wonderful plaster figures that it contains become animated in the ever-changing light, presenting them to the observer almost as living beings. The corner window was an invention of the modern movement in architecture; one thinks of Frank Lloyd Wright's Prairie houses and Gerrit Rietveld's Schroeder House, but Scarpa's imagination invested it with new meaning and value. Speaking about the project in 1978, Scarpa declared, 'I really love daylight: I wish I could frame the blue of the sky'. In this bejewelled building, he achieved that wish in full measure.

Figure 7.4 Carlo Scarpa, Museo Canoviano, Possagno, interior. (Gerry Johansson)

Buildings for all purposes

As one would expect, Louis Kahn was responsible for some of the most important contributions in reconciling the practicalities and poetics of daylight in architecture. Any of his mature buildings would serve to demonstrate this, and I have chosen the Yale Center for British Art (1969–1974) (Figure 7.5).[12] The building is an austere composition of exposed concrete frame, clad in stainless steel panels and lined with white plaster and panels of American oak. It was conceived to be daylit – 'a room is not a room without natural light' – and the entire roof plane is covered by a grid of square rooflights. The perimeter galleries and other spaces, including the library, are also lit by carefully dimensioned and positioned windows. Many of the paintings in the collection were painted to be hung in English country houses, and they depict English scenes viewed under the light of English skies. Kahn performs a remarkable trick by creating the illusion of just such a setting under the very different skies of Connecticut. The layered design of the rooflights, which have asymmetrical external louvres to exclude direct sunlight, and internal diffusion filters, subdues the bright light to render it appropriately subfusc as it plays on the restrained architecture of the interior. Kahn's extensive study drawings of the development of the rooflights show that these effects were the product of meticulous analysis. The measureable in the service of the unmeasurable.

Figure 7.5 Louis Kahn, Yale Center for British Art, interior. (Gerry Johansson)

A living master of imaginative light is Peter Zumthor. In the sequence of buildings that he has built in the last quarter of a century, he exhibits a special awareness of how the material of building may be fashioned to capture and project daylight in the service of their diverse uses. He has written,

> One of my favourite ideas is this: to plan the building as a pure mass of shadow then, afterwards to put in the light as if you were hollowing out the darkness, as if the light were a new mass seeping in.
>
> The second idea I like is this: to go about lighting materials and surfaces systematically and to look at the way in which they reflect the light. In other words, to choose the materials in the knowledge that they reflect and fit everything together on the basis of that knowledge.[13]

The translation of these ideas is wonderfully demonstrated in the Shelter for Roman Remains at Chur, completed in 1986 (Figure 7.6).[14] This deceptively simple building consists of three roof lit volumes that trace the outlines of the fragmentary remains of the Roman structure. The timber-framed form is clad with timber lamella and the zinc-covered roof is punctured by three

Figure 7.6 Peter Zumthor, Shelter for Roman Remains, Chur, interior. (Gerry Johansson)

large rooflights. But this tectonic simplicity conceals a deep and original understanding of the nature and behaviour of light. The walls are opaque to vision, but nonetheless transmit light by the process of inter-reflection through the lamellae. The effect is to cast a diffuse glow over the interior, the light warmed by the tone of the timber. This is then dramatised and transformed by the powerful zenithal light that cascades from the rooflights. The tall asymmetrical linings of the rooflight openings are, unusually, painted black and this starkly intensifies their light as it falls on the pale grey gravel of the floor. All of this is a clear demonstration of the architect's systematic, objective consideration of the interaction between light and material. The effect is spellbinding and original.

The codification of the environment in buildings evolved hand-in-glove with the development of the highly engineered building types of the twentieth century. The office building is, perhaps, the most familiar and, to some extent, the most successful case in which mechanical plant has become ubiquitous and artificial light has replaced daylight as the principal source of illumination, with many implications for environmental sustainability. There are, however, important exceptions to this rule. One such is the Heelis Building at Swindon in southern England (Figure 7.7). This is the headquarters of the National Trust, the custodian of much of England's architectural

Figure 7.7 Feilden Clegg Bradley Studios, Heelis Building, Swindon, exterior. (Gerry Johansson)

heritage; the building was completed in 2005 and is the work of architects Feilden Clegg Bradley Studios.[15]

The building is on the site of former railway works that were first developed by the great nineteenth-century engineer Isambard Kingdom Brunel. In its form, it refers to the pitched roofs of the original railway buildings. The deep plan is covered by a series of roof forms through which copious quantities of daylight enter and which promote natural ventilation throughout the building. They also support arrays of photovoltaic cells to generate valuable electricity. Beneath the roof, two-storey office spaces with mezzanines alternate with double-height communal and social spaces and the plan is penetrated by carefully positioned open-to-sky courts. The design intention is to provide natural light to all the workplaces by the simple strategy of ensuring that a direct view of the sky is seen from all positions. The standard, overcast 'design sky' used in quantitative design is three times brighter at the zenith than at the horizon. This means that 'skylight' is a better source than side lighting. In addition, it is a familiar empirical fact of daylighting under the English sky that a view of the sky provides adequate illumination for most practical purposes. The principles are elegantly applied and demonstrated at the Heelis building, where daylight factors range from 3 per cent beneath the mezzanine floors to an average of 9 per cent on the upper floor. In the double-height spaces, the light is allowed free rein and is animated by patches of sunlight that play over surfaces and materials and bring a dynamic connection with outside nature into the heart of this deep plan building. In its practicality and artfulness, the building becomes an appropriate symbol of the National Trust's mission.

Each of these buildings addresses specific and often specialised needs, be they acts of Christian worship, dwelling in the nineteenth-century city, the display and conservation of rare neo-classical sculpture, the public display of British art in North America, the protection of fragile Roman remains, or the practical and social needs of corporate headquarters. In each case, the objective need of shelter, protection and illumination are met, but what draws them to our attention here is the manner in which the ordinary is made extraordinary by acts of architectural imagination. However, this process is equally relevant in designing buildings that may be thought to be 'everyday'. To illustrate this, I conclude with a brief description of a small house that I built in the suburbs of Cambridge in 1991 (Figure 7.8). [16]

The house is a simple, single-storey structure in which all of the principal rooms connect with the courtyard garden. The living room is the largest and most complex space in the house. It is lit by south-facing windows and its most noticeable element is a tall bay window that lights the sitting area. At the latitude of Cambridge, 52° N, the sun's altitude at noon on the summer solstice is 62° and at the winter solstice is just 15°. The effect of this is to limit the penetration of the sun in summer to the edge of the room and, in winter, to penetrate its full depth. Inhabiting the room, one is in intimate contact with the progress of the seasons and the ever-changing light as the

Figure 7.8 Dean Hawkes, House at Cambridge, living room. (Dean Hawkes)

sun makes its daily passage from east to west. The spatial diversity of the room, with a low ceiling over the dining table and a high, curved vault above the sitting area, adds to the complexity of the light and to the enjoyment of the room.

There is almost no function in a building, institution, workplace or home, that may not be improved by being enacted in a place in which quantitative adequacy is complemented by carefully conceived gradations of light and shade, an awareness of the daily and seasonal cycles of the sun or the rich interplay between light and the form and materiality of a room. These are the tools by which we may bridge the space between Louis Kahn's measurable and unmeasurable. It is thus that buildings become works of architecture.

Notes

1 This essay is based on a paper given at the Velux Daylight Symposium 2011, held at the Rolex Centre, École Polytechnique Fédérale de Lausanne and published in *Daylight and Architecture*, Issue 15, Spring 2011, pp. 26–41.
2 Text inscription on drawing 'Architecture comes from the making of a room', signed 'Lou. K. 71'. Philadelphia Museum of Art. © Estate of Louis I. Kahn.
3 Louis I. Kahn, 'Silence and Light', lecture given at ETH, Zurich, 1969, in Heinz Ronner and Sharad Jahveri, *Louis I. Kahn: Complete Works*, Basel, Birkhäuser, 1987.

4 Dean Hawkes, *The Environmental Imagination: Technics and Poetics of the Architectural Environment*, London & New York, Routledge, 1st Edition, 2008, 2nd Edition, 2020.

5 Dean Hawkes, *Architecture and Climate: An Environmental History of British Architecture 1600–2000*, London & New York, Routledge, 2012.

6 See Dean Hawkes, 'Christopher Wren and the Origins of Building Science', in *Architecture and Climate*, op cit.

7 Kerry Downes, *A Thousand Years of the Church of St. Stephen Walbrook*, pamphlet, London, St. Stephen's Walbrook, undated.

8 Sir John Soane, Lecture VIII, *Sir John Soane: The Royal Academy Lectures*, David Watkin (Ed.), Cambridge, Cambridge University Press, 2000.

9 See Dean Hawkes, 'Soane, Labrouste, Mackintosh: Pioneers of Environment', in *The Environmental Imagination*, op cit.

10 Boris Podrecca, 'A Viennese Point of View', in Francesco dal Co and Giuseppe Mazzariol (Eds.), *Carlo Scarpa: The Complete Works*, Milan, Electa/London, The Architectural Press, 1986.

11 See Dean Hawkes, 'Carlo Scarpa, 'I Wish I Could Frame the Blue of the Sky'', in *The Environmental Imagination*, op cit.

12 See Dean Hawkes, 'Louis I. Kahn: The Poetics of Served and Servant', in *The Environmental Imagination*, op cit.

13 Peter Zumthor, 'A Way of Looking at Things', in Peter Zumthor, *Thinking Architecture*, Basel, Birkhäuser, 1999.

14 See Dean Hawkes, 'The Sheltering Environment', in *The Environmental Imagination*, op cit.

15 Ian Latham and Mark Swennarton (Eds.), *Feilden Clegg Bradley: The Environmental Handbook*, London, Right Angle Publishing, 2007.

16 Marcus Field, 'Building Study: Hawkes House, Cambridge', *The Architects' Journal*, 7 March, 1996, pp. 37–41.

Essay 8[1]
The selective environment
Environmental design and cultural identity

Introduction

> [T]he main antagonist of rooted culture is the ubiquitous air-conditioner. Wherever they occur, the fixed window and the air-conditioner are mutually indicative of domination by universal technique.
> *– Kenneth Frampton, 1983*

In this statement, Kenneth Frampton[2] identifies the air-conditioner as a potent symbol of the way in which the environmental function of architecture was transformed during the later decades of the twentieth century. Through the agency of mechanical systems, operating within sealed building envelopes, Le Corbusier's proposition of 'only one house for all countries, the house of *exact breathing*' has become globally commonplace.[3]

But, in contrast to this powerful stereotype, we have seen the emergence of a strong and alternative line of thought. This rests upon the case for a *regionally* grounded approach to contemporary design that was argued so eloquently by Frampton. In its environmental manifestation, the regionalist position was probably first presented by Victor Olgyay in 1963 in *Design with Climate: Bioclimatic Approach to Architectural Regionalism*.[4] More recent and continuing advocacy for regionalism, in a wide interpretation, has come from Alexander Tzonis and Lianne Lefaivre in a sequence of important publications.[5] The idea of *The Selective Environment* originated in work at Cambridge University in the UK and is located within the regionalist paradigm and proposes a broad strategy for design that embraces both the technical and the cultural in the realisation of a sustainable architecture.[6]

Definitions

In *The Architecture of the Well-tempered Environment* Reyner Banham proposed three distinct 'modes' of environmental control that may be applied in architecture.[7] He named them the 'Conservative', the 'Selective' and the 'Regenerative'. Banham's classification was derived from the empirical observation of historical building types and effectively served the needs of his essentially historical analysis. In 1980, the present author adapted

DOI: 10.4324/9781003083023-9

Table 8.1 General characteristics of Exclusive and Selective mode buildings

Exclusive Mode	Selective Mode
Environment is automatically controlled and is predominantly artificial.	*Environment* is controlled by a combination of automatic and manual means and is a variable mixture of the natural and artificial.
Shape is compact, seeking to minimise the interface between interior and exterior environments.	*Shape* is dispersed, seeking to maximise the potential collection and use of ambient energy.
Orientation is disregarded.	*Orientation* is carefully observed.
Windows are generally restricted in size.	*Window* sizes are related to the dimensions of internal spaces and to orientation of façades.
Energy is primarily from remote generated sources and is in constant use throughout	*Energy* is a combination of ambient – solar, and wind – and externally generated sources.
	The use varies seasonally, with peak demand in winter and 'free-running' operation in summer.

Dean Hawkes, 'Building Shape and Energy Use', in Dean Hawkes and Janet Owers (Eds.), *The Architecture of Energy*, London, Longman & Co., 1980.

Banham's categories in order to a make a clear distinction in environmental design strategies that could be observed in contemporary design practice. This defined two modes of environmental control, the 'Exclusive' and the 'Selective', whose principal characteristics are summarised in Table 8.1.

These modes correspond precisely to the distinction between the *global* (Exclusive) and the *regional* (Selective). In a later representation it was acknowledged that, in addition to these quite precisely defined modes, there is a large and uncharted body of buildings in which environmental design is, regrettably, more a matter of chance than intention. This was presented in an adaptation of Ebenezer Howard's 'Three Magnets' diagram from the Garden City Movement that describes this category as the 'Pragmatic' mode (Figure 8.1).

The original work on the definition of the 'Selective' mode was based upon an analysis of the environmental conditions of the temperate regions of the northern hemisphere, where seasonal differences are marked and where distinctions of orientation are of significance in design. Later work sought to extend and generalise the application of 'Selective' principles to the global scale. This led to a comprehensive restatement of the principles in which the significance of accounting for local climate and regional practices is emphasised (Table 8.2).

Nature and architecture

The relationship between the external climate and the internal environments of buildings lies at the heart of the distinction between the 'Exclusive' and

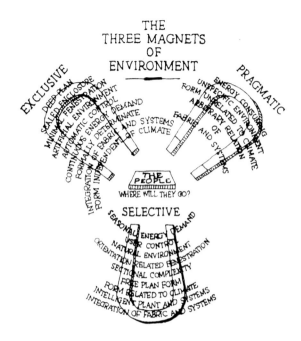

Figure 8.1 'Three Magnets of Environment'. (Dean Hawkes)

Table 8.2 Global characteristics of Selective mode buildings

Internal environment	Standards are related to the local climate. Emphasis is upon the maximisation of natural light. There is spatial and temporal diversity of environmental conditions. Control is primarily by the occupant.
Built form	Related to the specific climate. Influenced by regional practice. Cross-section a key instrument of environmental response.
Orientation	Related to the specific climate. Influenced by regional practice. Knowledge of solar geometry (sun path) is essential.
Fenestration	Related to the specific climate. Influenced by regional practice. Window design must balance the relationship between the thermal and luminous environments.
Energy sources	Energy should be primarily from ambient sources: exploiting natural light, useful solar gains and natural ventilation where appropriate. Mechanical systems for heating/cooling, ventilation and lighting should be considered as supplementary to the primary function of selective built form. Make direct use of renewable energy by the use of water-heating and photovoltaic systems.

Dean Hawkes, Jane McDonald and Koen Steemers. *The Selective Environment: An Approach to Environmentally Responsive Architecture*, London, The Spon Press, 2002.

'Selective' modes of environmental control. In discussing the 'contingencies of climate and temporally inflected qualities of local light', Kenneth Frampton has written,

> The generic window is obviously the most delicate point at which these two forces impinge upon the outer membrane of the building, fenestration having an innate capacity to inscribe architecture with the character of a region and hence to express the place in which the work is situated.[8]

The key strategy of 'Exclusive' design is to minimise the interaction between the naturally occurring external climate and the environment within a building. The combination of a sealed envelope and mechanical and electrical service systems allows, perhaps requires, the internal environment to be almost entirely artificial. Nature is held at bay in the interests of notions of 'precision' of control and 'efficiency' of operation, machines have taken over the environmental function. But, until that moment at some point in the twentieth century at which this separation was first realised, all architecture had been fundamentally concerned to enter into a kind of treaty with the natural environment in order to achieve conditions under which the needs – practical, cultural and symbolic – of humankind could be met. In that sense, all of these buildings were environmentally 'Selective'.

The success of this strategy can be amply demonstrated through the built evidence of architectural history. Buildings for all purposes, through their form, construction and detail, become a kind of representation – a *register* – of the conditions within which they were created. The Pantheon at Rome (126 AD, 42°N) (Figure 8.2) demonstrates a deep understanding of the brightness of the sky and its potential to illuminate a large volume of space. In Christopher Wren's library at Trinity College, Cambridge (52°N), completed in 1695, (Figure 8.3) the proportional relationship between the windows, set high in the walls, and the cross-section of the space ideally lights both books and readers. Some two centuries later, Henri Labrouste followed this model in his design for the Bibliotèque Ste. Geneviève in Paris (1838–1850, 49°N) (Figure 8.4). Although, by this date, the technologies of both structural engineering and of space heating had developed considerably and found their place in the building, the environmental form in the heart of Paris is close to that of the precedent on the banks of the River Cam. The diversity of the fenestration of Charles Rennie Mackintosh's Glasgow School of Art (1896–1909, 56°N) (Figure 8.5) is evidence of the complex relationships that occur between the functional requirements and the internal organisation of a building such as this and the external urban environment in which it is located.[9] It is interesting to note that among the many windows on the south side there are a number of louvred grilles that serve the building's extensive ventilation system.

Figure 8.2 Pantheon, Rome. (Alamy)

Figure 8.3 Christopher Wren, Library, Trinity College, Cambridge, west front. (Dean Hawkes)

Figure 8.4 Henri Labrouste, Bibliotèque Ste. Genevieve, Paris. (iStock)

Figure 8.5 Charles Rennie Mackintosh, Glasgow School of Art, north façade. (Ranald Lawrence)

Figure 8.6 Erik Gunnar Asplund, Gothenburg Law Courts. (Dean Hawkes)

This connection between inside and outside environments continued to inform much architecture of significance throughout the twentieth century. In the Scandinavian tradition and the northern latitudes, the works of Erik Gunnar Asplund and Alvar Aalto consistently reveal an acute understanding of nature and its specific manifestation in climate.[10] Asplund's extension to the Gothenburg Law Courts (57°N) (Figure 8.6) shows this sensibility at work in the heart of the city and Aalto's Saynatsalo Town Hall (62°N) (Figure 8.7) is beautifully adapted to its context on a wooded island. In both buildings the cross-section is a key element in controlling the interaction between interior and exterior, and orientation is a controlling factor in response to the sun's low trajectory across the northern sky.

As a final demonstration, consider the works of Louis I. Kahn. The Kimbell Art Museum at Fort Worth (1966–1972) (Figure 8.8) and the Yale Center for British Art at New Haven (1969–1974) (Figure 7.5), illustrate the application of consistent principles in designing buildings for almost identical purposes, but are located in quite different climates – Texas and Connecticut, at latitudes of 33°N and 41°N, respectively. As in the works of Asplund and Aalto, the cross-section plays a vital role, but the formal outcomes, one building with the emphasis on shading the interior from the brightness and heat of the Texan skies, the other more transparent to more temperate skies, are radically different from each other and from the works of the Scandinavian masters.[11]

Figure 8.7 Alvar Aalto, Saynatsalo Town Hall. (Dean Hawkes)

All of these examples show that, across centuries and continents, buildings have used form and materiality to connect and transform the relationship between the external and internal climates. The argument here is that this strategy lies at the heart of architecture, as both a technical and cultural enterprise. When this link is severed by the imposition of a sealed envelope and the introduction of environmental machines, something of the essence of architecture is forfeited. But it is vital to stress that 'Selective' design is not a reactionary strategy. As needs and techniques have evolved, the potentiality of new circumstances has led to new solutions to old problems and the discovery of appropriate solutions to new needs.

Writing of Louis Kahn's Yale Art Gallery (1951–1953), Vincent Scully referred to the 'sombre and archaic tension' that he found in the design.[12] This judgement might be also applied to the works of Kahn's last years. The Kimbell Art Museum is lit by an aperture at the apex of a vault, as is the Pantheon, but Kimbell is entirely a building of its time, adopting the technologies of the twentieth century in meeting the stringent environmental needs of the modern art museum. By the standards and practices of the time, this involved the installation of air-conditioning, but this finds its place within a conception of the building envelope that is rooted in the historical

Figure 8.8 Louis Kahn, Kimbell Art Museum, Fort Worth, Texas. (Dean Hawkes)

method of architecture. It is from this that Scully's 'sombre and archaic tension' derives.

Comfort and climate

> As life has arisen through the hidden aspects of natural laws, so for better or worse the rules of nature command that life make a close adjustment to natural background. The setting is impartial, it can be cruel or kind, but all living species must either adapt their physiology through selection or mutations or find other defences against the impact of the environment.[13]

The mechanisation of environmental control that is represented by the 'Exclusive' mode presupposes that human comfort is a matter of narrow, quantified standards of heat, light and sound and that these standards are universal or global. The 'Selective' environment, however, is founded on an alternative approach in which comfort is acknowledged to be a complex phenomenon that involves spatial and temporal variation and both long- and short-term adaptation by the occupants of buildings.

A key development in research into the theoretical basis of environmental design has been the idea of the 'adaptive' model. This has its origins in work published in the 1970s by Michael Humphreys, who undertook some seminal studies at the Building Research Establishment in the United Kingdom.[14] This pioneering work has been considerably developed and extended by Humphreys in collaboration with Fergus Nicol and Susan Roaf in two volumes on, *Adaptive Thermal Comfort*.[15] The principles of adaptive thermal comfort were succinctly stated by Humphreys in an earlier paper.[16] In this he demonstrated that people take a variety of actions to secure comfort in buildings proposing that, 'If change occurs such as to produce discomfort, people tend to react in ways which tend to restore comfort'. Within this philosophy Humphreys made a number of specific proposals for design action that are the basis of adaptive comfort. These coincide with the broad principles of 'Selective' design where the actions of the 'users' of a building are fundamental to the idea.[17] Humphreys' adaptive principles may be paraphrased as follows:

- The environment should be predictable: the occupants should know what to expect.
- The environment should be 'normal': it should be within the range acceptable in the social circumstances in that society and climate.
- The environment should provide thermal variety, where this is appropriate.
- Where people must be at a fixed location in the building, they should have adequate control of their immediate environment.
- Sudden changes of temperature should be avoided.

Humphreys has shown that there is a strong correlation between ambient temperatures and acceptable indoor conditions. His work also suggests that people are more tolerant of conditions in what he terms 'free-running' buildings – characteristic of 'Selective' designs – than in those with the mechanically controlled environments provided by 'Exclusive' design. The significance of Humphreys' work and its development with his collaborators in the literature of *Adaptive Thermal Cooling*, is its explicit demonstration that environmental conditions within buildings should be, within limits, spatially and temporally diverse and that there is strong evidence that environmental expectations are related to prevailing regional conditions.

Exemplars of 'selective' design

A 'Selective' building, by definition, enjoys an intimate relationship with its immediate environment. That environment is explicitly and objectively characterised by the physical description of the local climate and by the set of parameters by which 'adaptive' comfort might be achieved. However, these parameters are always subject to elaboration and interpretation in the light of the cultural pressures that are crucial to the production of a work of architecture. Whilst many important facts about buildings can be presented in the formulations of building science, these inevitably remain in the realm of the abstract. One of the most potent ways in which architectural knowledge is transmitted is by reference to specific building instances. Here it is possible to address the complex relationships of the technological and the cultural. This essay is concluded by examining a sequence of 'exemplars', drawn from global practice, that indicate something of the potential of the idea. They are presented in two groups. The first, appeared in the paper as first published in 2001, the second group are drawn from more recent global practice.

Group 1

Library, Darwin College, University of Cambridge, Cambridge, UK. Architects: Jeremy Dixon and Edward Jones, 1994, 52°N.[18] (Figure 8.9)

Any new building in the core of a historic city carries obligations to its setting, so the form and language of the building must demonstrate a specific response to the unique conditions of the site and programme. Here a narrow site on the banks of River Cam, close to the city centre, not far from Christopher Wren's library at Trinity College, and to the existing nineteenth- and twentieth-century buildings of the college, is occupied by a building that responds to orientation and context, to create a naturally lit and ventilated

Figure 8.9 Jeremy Dixon and Edward Jones, Library, Darwin College, Cambridge. (Dean Hawkes)

environment for study. In absolute accordance with 'Selective' principles, the 'secret' lies in the cross-section. A rebuilt garden wall becomes the north face of the building towards a busy street and the two-storey arrangement within provides a variety of working places that face south over the river. At the upper level, a range of windows admit abundant daylight and include user-operated opening lights for natural ventilation. They also admit useful solar warmth in the heating season. High level clerestorey windows provide additional illumination and combine with a tall vent chimney to supply fresh air and summer cooling.

Strawberry Vale School, Victoria, British Columbia, Canada. Architects: Patkau, 1995, 48°N. (Figure 8.10)

The Canadian architects, Patkau, consistently address environmental questions in their work. Strawberry Vale Elementary School in Victoria adds to the long line of school designs that, from the nineteenth century, occupy a key place in the history of environmental architecture.[19] Once again, the cross-section is the key to the environmental strategy in clearly allowing and environmental response to the educational programme – low, south-facing spaces for classrooms, tall spaces at the centre of the plan for shared resources and service rooms to the north.

Figure 8.10 Patkau Architects, Strawberry Vale School, Victoria, British Columbia. (Patkau Architects)

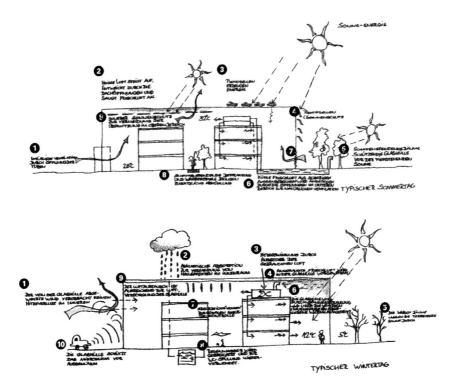

Figure 8.11 Jourda et Perraudin, Mont Cenis Training Centre, Herne-Sodingen. (Jourda Architectes/Gilles Perraudin Architecte)

Mont Cenis Training Centre, Herne-Sodingen, Germany. Architects: Jourda et Perraudin, 1997, 52°N. (Figure 8.11)[20]

This was one of the most environmentally radical buildings from the last years of the twentieth century. It adopts an all-enveloping primary structure that provides the first degree of environmental selection with a translucent skin that admits natural light, but provides weatherproofing, temperature modification and, through the provision of photovoltaic cells, energy production. Buildings for a wide range of public functions are located within the sheltered microclimate created by this enclosure, which also becomes the setting for a range of civic and social activities.

Shelter for Roman Remains, Chur, Switzerland. Architect: Peter Zumthor, 1986, 46.9°N. (Figure 7.6)[21]

This building shows how, in certain, specialised circumstances, it is possible to make a modern building that relies entirely on the building enclosure to meet the environmental demands of the programme. It is a simple timber structure that encloses and protects the remains of a group of Roman buildings. The enclosure dramatises the ancient fabric by contrasting the warm

Figure 8.12 Glenn Murcutt, Arthur and Yvonne Boyd Art Centre, Riverdale, NSW. (Luke Butterly)

glow diffused through the louvred walls with the strong zenithal illumination of the two rooflights. The glazing of these slopes to the north excludes direct sunlight from the lower levels. The space is continuously ventilated through the walls. This is a unique and original illustration of the principles of 'Selective' design.

Arthur and Yvonne Boyd Art Centre, Riverdale, West Cambewarra, NSW, Australia. Architect: Glenn Murcutt. 1999, 35°S. (Figure 8.12)[22]

Glenn Murcutt's singular practise in Australia has produced a long sequence of environmentally responsive buildings that reinterpret the building traditions and environmental conditions of Australia through the experience of architectural modernism. Françoise Fromonot has observed that,

> 'Murcutt continues to attach an analysis of natural phenomena to aesthetic implications – to ally the scientific with the picturesque'.[23]

The great majority of Murcutt's buildings are houses, but in a number of designs for larger buildings he demonstrates how the principles that he has explored in these small buildings may be effectively translated to the larger scale. The Arthur and Yvonne Boyd Art Centre is a clear illustration of this. Set in a beautiful landscape, the building evinces numerous specific responses to climate and topography. The oversailing roof that is characteristic of Murcutt's works is the primary element of environmental response,

Figure 8.13 Abhikram Architects with Brian Ford, Torrent Research Centre, Ahmedabad. (Brian Ford)

beneath which the specific environmental needs of the diverse functions are finely calibrated by 'Selective' means.

The Torrent Research Centre, Ahmedabad, India. Architects: Abhikram with Brian Ford, 2000, 23°N. (Figure 8.13)

This research laboratory at Ahmedabad is the outcome of collaboration between the Indian architects Abhikram and the British architect-environmentalist Brian Ford.[24] The significance of this group of buildings lies in the application of principles of natural cooling, ventilation and lighting in a building type that conventionally is dependent upon mechanical methods of environmental control. In addition, it achieves this in a hot climate that is inherently hostile. As is usual with these designs the key lies in the cross-section. This shows the arrays of tall ventilation towers that rise above the sides of the buildings and the central atrium space that also extends above roof level. These promote the ventilation that maintains the internal environment. They are, perhaps, 'Selective' design's equivalent of Louis Kahn's service towers at the Richards Medical Research Building in Philadelphia – Kahn's 'served' and 'servant' reinterpreted for the new era. This environmental strategy has a profound influence on the form of the buildings and becomes a potent symbol of both their technology and ideology.

Group 2 – the twenty-first century

The Ger Innovation Hub, Ulaanbaatar, Mongolia. Architects: Rural Urban Framework, Hong Kong University (HKU), 2019, Latitude 48°N. (Figure 8.14)

This small building is as simple as can be and serves to illustrate the application of 'selective' principles in a context that is unique and challenging in the 21st century.[25] In recent years the capital city of Mongolia has experienced rapid urban growth around its perimeter. Much of this has been in the form of traditional residential gers, with little supporting infrastructure. The Innovation Hub was designed by Rural Urban Framework, a research and design laboratory at HKU, and provides space for elementary education and as a social space for the wider community. The building combines an inner core of four L-shaped, mud block walls that define an irregular cruciform space enclosing a shallow sunken amphitheatre, surrounded by an irregular heptagonal glazed enclosure. This defines a central, environmentally stable area with the perimeter serving as a buffer zone with more variable environments.

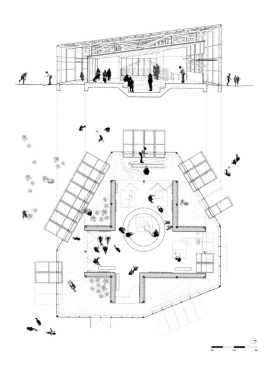

Figure 8.14 Rural Urban Framework, The Ger Innovation Hub, Ulaanbaatar, Mongolia. (Rural Urban Framework, Hong Kong University)

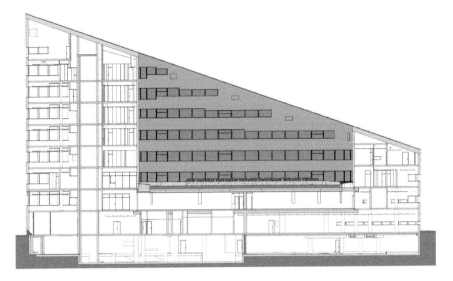

Figure 8.15 Snøhetta, Powerhouse Office Building, Brattørkaia, Trondheim. (Snøhetta)

Powerhouse Office Building, Brattørkaia, Trondheim, Norway. Architects: Snøhetta, 2019, 63.5°N. (Figure 8.15)

The office building could be said to be the most successful building type of the modern era. In particular the glass skyscraper with a sealed glass envelope and full mechanical services that is the direct descendent of Mies van der Rohe's projects for sites in Berlin of 1919 and 1921. Such buildings dominate the skylines of major cities around the globe as a demonstration of the dominance of 'universal technique' over 'rooted culture', in Frampton's terminology.[26] Those buildings are designed for resistance to the diverse climates in which they are located. In contrast the Powerhouse at Trondheim in Norway is designed by architects Snøhetta according to the principle 'form follows the environment'.[27] The building has an irregular trapezoidal plan that is penetrated by an elliptical, open-to-sky courtyard that is orientated on the cardinal point diagonally across the plan. The cross-section reduces in height across the diagonal, from north to south in response to the passage of the sun. The entire roof surface and those upper areas of the façades that receive a high level of insolation are clad in photovoltaic collectors. These produce a net positive energy balance for the annual cycle, offsetting imported energy needed in the winter months. The courtyard plan ensures that the office floors have good natural light. Heating and ventilation are by mechanical plant, but this is designed to operate efficiently in the often-harsh climate of this far-northern city.

Figure 8.16 Mario Cucinella Architects, ARPEA Regional Agency Building, Ferrara.
(Moreno Maggi)

*ARPAE Regional Agency Building, Ferrara, Italy. Architects: Mario
Cucinella Architects, 2015, 45°N.* (Figure 8.16)

Moving from the high latitude of Norway, 65.5°N, to northern Italy at
Ferrara, at 45°N, another design for an office building applies similar environmental principles to the very different climate. Located on a site on the
edge of the historic city, the building is the headquarters of ARPEA, an
environmental agency. The work of Mario Cucinella Architects, the timber-
constructed, single-storey building is based on a rectangular grid of top-lit
elements that are interpenetrated by open-to-sky courtyards, or winter gar-
dens.[28] The rectangular elements, 'chimney forms' in the architects' terminology, serve to admit and distribute sunlight and daylight through the deep plan
and to promote natural ventilation by stack effect. Alternate skylights have
photovoltaic cells that produce energy for the building services. The building
responds to the distinct seasons of the climate of the Po Valley, with cool,
humid winters and hot, humid summers, by changing the function of the
chimneys. In the summer, air is expelled through these to avoid stratification
of air, and in winter, they act as solar collectors operating with a heat recov-
ery system. The elegantly detailed, timber-clad structure that hovers above
the office spaces, subtly expresses the environmental logic of the building as
a further demonstration of the principle of 'form follows environment'.

*Lambeth Palace Library, London, UK. Architects: Wright and Wright,
2021, 51.5°N.* (Figure 8.17)

It is implicit in the principles of selective design that effective, environmentally responsive design may be realised by a process of architectural
evolution. That precedent may be transformed by new knowledge and
technology. The library at Lambeth Palace, the official residence of the

Figure 8.17 Wright and Wright. Lambeth Palace Library, London. (Hufton & Crow/VIEW)

Archbishop of Canterbury in London, by Wright and Wright Architects is an eloquent demonstration of this.[29] The site is at the edge of the garden of the historic palace, close to the banks of River Thames. The library houses some 200,000 books and manuscripts, many of which are of historical significance. Their protection and conservation were a primary objective in the new building and a key component of the environmental brief. The building is in the form of a central nine-storey tower flanked by wings of five and four storeys. The ground and first floors house the principal public spaces for administration, a conservation studio and the public reading room. Above the entire building is given to the archive that occupies the upper levels of the wings and the tower, with the exception of the eighth floor, where there is a seminar room and open terrace giving views across London.

The environmental strategy derives from and supports the functional organisation of the building. All the public areas are daylit with, in most cases, views over the palace garden. On the other hand, the archive floors are windowless to provide a stable environment for their precious contents. The engineering consultant describes these as a hybrid design in which temperature and humidity is allowed to vary seasonally within limits, with fine-tuning provided by mechanical plant. The brick-clad envelope has a high level of thermal insulation and the extensive roofs of the two lower wings are covered in photovoltaic cells that supply power for the electrical systems. In its fundamentals the building respects the principles that have informed the environmental response of architecture to the British climate throughout its history,[30] but addressing the new priorities of the 21st century by the application of new standards, principles and technologies.

Postscript

In conclusion, I return to Kenneth Frampton's analysis with which I began, with its distinction between the *global* – universal technique – and the *regional* – rooted culture. My aim in selecting these exemplars of 'Selective' design has been to show that the principles do not lead to uniformity, but that observance of the specific conditions of climate, building traditions and culture of a place can produce architecture that addresses the environmental priorities of the twenty-first century without sacrifice of the sense of continuity and innovation that has informed the production of architecture throughout its history. In this we may achieve a collaboration between the universal science of building that provides objective understanding of the physical forces at play and the regional interpretation of building traditions and practices that connect design to the implications of the underlying culture.

Notes

1 This essay is an extended version of a paper first published in the *Proceedings of the iNTA Conference*, Singapore, 2001.
2 Kenneth Frampton, 'Towards a Critical Regionalism: Six Points for an Architecture of Resistance', in Hal Foster (Ed.), *Postmodern Culture*, London & Concord, MA, Pluto Press, 1983, pp. 18–30.
3 Le Corbusier, *Precisions on the Present State of Architecture and the City*, Paris, Crès et Cie, 1930, English translation, Boston, MA, MIT Press, 1991.
4 Victor Olgyay, *Design with Climate: Bioclimatic Approach to Architectural Regionalism*, Princeton, NJ, Princeton University Press, 1963, 2nd Edition, 2015.
5 Alexander Tzonis, Lianne Lefaivre and Bruno Stagno, *Tropical Architecture: Critical Regionalism in the Age of Globalization*, Chichester, Wiley-Academy, 2001; Lianne Lefaivre and Alexander Tzonis, *Critical Regionalism: Architecture and Identity in a Globalized World*, Munich & London, Prestel, 2003; Alexander Tzonis and Lianne Lefaivre, *Architecture of Regionalism in the Age of Globalization*, London & New York, Routledge, 2012.
6 Dean Hawkes, Jane McDonald and Koen Steemers, *The Selective Environment: An Approach to Environmentally Responsive Architecture*, London, The Spon Press, 2002.
7 Reyner Banham, *The Architecture of the Well-Tempered Environment*, London, The Architectural Press, 1969, 2nd Edition, Chicago, IL, Chicago University Press, 1984.
8 Kenneth Frampton, 'Towards a Critical Regionalism', op cit, pp. 18–30.
9 Glasgow, as so many industrial cities in the nineteenth century, suffered from a heavily polluted microclimate. The impact of this on Mackintosh's design is explored in depth in Ranald Lawrence, *The Victorian Art School: Architecture, History and Environment*, Abingdon & New York, Routledge, 2020.

10 This topic is explored at length in Dean Hawkes, *The Environmental Imagination: Technics and Poetics of the Architectural Environment*, Abingdon & New York, Routledge, 1st Edition, 2008, 2nd Edition, 2020.

11 The environments of Kahn's buildings are also discussed in Dean Hawkes, *The Environmental Imagination*, op cit.

12 Vincent Scully, 'Sombre and Archaic: Expressive Tension', *Yale Daily News*, 6 November 1953.

13 Victor Olgyay, *Design with Climate*, op cit.

14 M.A. Humphreys, 'Field Studies of Thermal Comfort Compared and Applied', *Building Research Establishment Current Paper, CP 76/75*, Garston, BRE, 1975, pp. 1–12; M.A. Humphreys, 'The Influence of Season and Ambient Temperature on Human Clothing Behaviour', in P.O. Fanger and O. Valbjorn (Eds.), *Indoor Climate*, Copenhagen, Danish Building Research Institute, 1978. M.A. Humphreys, 'Outdoor Temperatures and Comfort Indoors', *Building Research and Practice*, Vol. 6, No. 2, 1978, p. 92.

15 Fergus Nicol, Michael Humphreys and Susan Roaf, *Adaptive Thermal Comfort: Principles and Practice*, Abingdon & New York, Routledge, 2012. Michael Humphrey, Fergus Nicol and Susan Roaf, *Adaptive Thermal Comfort: Foundations and Analysis*, Abingdon & New York, Routledge, 2020.

16 See, Michael Humphreys, 'What Causes Discomfort?', in *Workplace Comfort Forum*, London, RIBA, 1995; and 'An Adaptive Approach to Thermal Comfort Criteria', in Derek Clements-Croome (Ed.), *Naturally Ventilated Building: Buildings for the Senses, the Economy and Society*, London & New York, E. & F.N. Spon, 1997, pp. 129–137. Other contemporary work occurred simultaneously in Cambridge. See Nick Baker and Mark Standeven, 'Adaptive Opportunity as a Comfort Parameter', in *Workplace Comfort Forum*, op cit, and Nick Baker, 'The Irritable Occupant: Recent Developments in Thermal Comfort Theory', *Architectural Research Quarterly*, Vol. 2, 1996, pp. 84–90.

17 This was outlined in Dean Hawkes, 'The Theoretical Basis of Comfort in 'Selective' Environments', *Energy and Buildings*, Vol. 5, No. 2, December 1982, pp. 127–134; reprinted in Dean Hawkes, *The Environmental Tradition: Studies in the Architecture of Environment*, London & New York, E. & F.N. Spon, 1996, pp. 28–35.

18 For a description of the building see, Ian Latham and Mark Swenarton (Eds.), *Jeremy Dixon and Edward Jones: Buildings and Projects 1959–2002*, London, Right Angle Publishing, 2002. For a specifically environmental description, see Dean Hawkes and Wayne Forster, *Architecture, Engineering, Environment*, London, Lawrence King, 2002.

19 See Dean Hawkes, 'The Historical Context', in Peter Clegg (Ed.), *Feilden Clegg Bradley Studios: Learning From Schools*, London, Artifice Books on Architecture, 2015, pp. 8–17.

20 See Dean Hawkes and Wayne Forster, *Architecture, Engineering, Environment*, op cit.

21 The environmental qualities of this building are discussed in Dean Hawkes, *The Environmental Imagination*, op cit.

22 See Françoise Fromonot, *Glenn Murcutt: Buildings and Projects, 1962–2003*, London & New York, Thames and Hudson, 2003.

23 Ibid.

24 The building is described in detail in Brian Ford, Rosa Schiano-Phan and Juan A. Vallejo, *The Architecture of Natural Cooling*, 2nd Edition, London & New York, Routledge, 2020.

25 See Bilegt Baasandavaa, 'Becoming Urban', *The Architectural Review*, October, 2020, pp. 20–26.

26 Kenneth Frampton, 'Towards a Critical Regionalism', op cit.

27 From website https://www.powerhouse.no/prosjekter/brattorkaia, accessed 16 March 2021.

28 See Anna Mainoli (Ed.), *Mario Cucinella Architects: Building Green Futures*, Florence, Forma Edizioni S.r.l., 2020.

29 Rolfe Kentish, 'Building Study: Lambeth Palace Library', *Architecture Today*, Issue 311, January-February 2021, pp. 30–38.

30 See Dean Hawkes, *Architecture and Climate: An Environmental History of British Architecture: 1600–2000*, London & New York, Routledge, 2012.

Essay 9[1]
The technical imagination
Thoughts on the relation of technique and design in architecture

Introduction

As a practising architect, as a teacher of both design studio and, for many years, of technical subjects, I have been engaged with the question of the status of building technique in the conception and realisation of buildings. In this essay I shall try to outline some of the thoughts that I have had over the years and, from these, to draw out some implications for the teaching of technical matters in schools of architecture.

First, I should explain my title. This comes from the painter, Francis Bacon (1909-1992), who wrote,

> Real imagination is *technical imagination* (my italics). It is the ways in which you think up to bring an event to life again. It is in the search for the technique to trap the object at a given moment. Then the technique and object become inseparable. The object is the technique and the technique is the object.[2]

I am attracted by this because it emphatically establishes a connection between technique and creativity. It asserts that the two are in some way interdependent, they 'become inseparable'. Consequently, I propose that questions of technique should be at the centre of education and practice in architecture and not be consigned to some peripheral and, hence, secondary status.

Next, I should explain my avoidance of the word *technology*, and my preference for *technique*. The *Oxford English Dictionary* defines the difference between the terms as following from the distinction between science *(technology)* and art *(technique)*.[3] I find the separation of the territories of art and science as it is, or may be, applied to architecture – and to architectural education – extremely troubling. While there is clearly some credibility in the familiar view that architecture is a combination of art and science, I believe that many problems follow from this. Primarily these are problems of division and reduction, which seems to me to contradict the fundamental nature of architecture as synthesis. On the other hand, my preference for

DOI: 10.4324/9781003083023-10

technique over *technology* should not be taken to imply a rejection of science and objectivity in architecture. My intention is, rather, to connect the technical dimension of design to all of the other questions, of the conception of space, of composition, of functional organisation, which are also matters of technique, but which are manifestly not matters of technology.

Technique and design

Turning now to more specifically architectural questions, I want to examine two different propositions about the place of technical matters in architectural theory. In his book, *The Architecture of Humanism* published in 1914,[4] Geoffrey Scott wrote, 'The relation of construction to design is the fundamental problem of architectural aesthetics'.

In the light of what I have said above it is clear why I find this an attractive statement in its assertion of the *fundamental* position of construction – in which I suggest we can include all those aspects of design which we deem to be technical – in the discourse of architectural aesthetics. In fact, Scott's purpose, in his attack on what he defines as *The Mechanical Fallacy*, was to contradict the Ruskinian argument deriving from his (Ruskin's) devotion to the Gothic, of the status of construction in determining the very essence of buildings and to argue that architecture is most fundamentally, 'a combination, revealed through light and shade, of masses and of lines'.

From this, Scott went on to argue that the surest means by which these objectives may be realised is through the classical tradition of architecture and, in particular through the lessons of the buildings of the Renaissance.

> To pass from Roman architecture or that of the Renaissance to the fantastic and bewildered energy of Gothic, is to leave humanism for magic. The study of the congruous for the cult of the strange. It is to find that the logic of an inhuman science has displaced the logic of the human form. It is to discover resplendent beauty of detail in glass and bronze and ivory and gold; it is to lose architecture in sculpture. Here is structure, certainly – daring, intricate, ingenious, but seldom humanised structure. Here is poetry, curious craftsmanship, exquisite invention. But the supreme, the distinctive quality of architecture – that pure identity between the inner and the outer world – is unattempted.

Scott's argument has to be seen in the context of the debate in British architecture at the turn of the century, in which the nineteenth century's 'Battle of the Styles' was reaching its climax, and to some extent its resolution, in the conflict between the inheritors of the tradition of Ruskin and Pugin in the 'Free School' and the academic tradition of revived classicism. As Robert Macleod showed in his book, *Style and Society*[5], this was given particular focus by the move at the turn of the century towards the formal education of architects in full-time schools, in place of the pupillage system that was previously the

principal route of entry into the profession. With its connotations of mediaeval guilds, pupillage was at the very heart of 'Free School' practice and was
thus difficult to reconcile with the idea of academic education. In the event,
the hiatus of the First World War diffused the debate, but the fact remains that
the majority of the British schools were founded on the academic tradition,
derived in its academic structure from the Beaux Arts. In this respect we may
conclude that, at this crucial moment in the development of architecture in
Britain, the primarily academic and aesthetic arguments of Scott and his like
triumphed over the pragmatic and craft-based position of the Ruskinian line.

Not long after the publication of Scott's book a very different point of
view was argued about the status of technical matters in the production of
architecture. In 1920, Le Corbusier declared his *Cinque points d'une architecture nouvelle* in the journal *L'Esprit Nouveau*.[6] In 1929, he elaborated the
theme when he delivered a series of ten lectures in Buenos Aires.[7] The second
of these had the title, 'Techniques are the very basis of poetry'. (Figure 9.1)

Ladies and Gentlemen, I begin by drawing a line that can separate, in
the process of our perceptions, the domain of material things, daily

Figure 9.1 Le Corbusier, 'Techniques are the very basis of poetry'. (FLC/ADAGP,
Paris, DACS, London 2021)

events, reasonable tendencies, from that specially reserved to spiritual ones. Below the line, *what exists*, above, *what one feels*. (My italics)

Continuing my drawing from the bottom, I draw one, two, three plates. I put something in each plate. In the first: *technique*, a general word lacking precision, but which I qualify rapidly by these terms that bring us back to our subject: *resistance of materials, chemistry, physics*.

In the second plate I write: *sociology*.

In the third plate: *economics*.

I step over the line and enter the domain of the emotions. I draw a pipe and the smoke of a pipe. And then a little bird who flies off, and, in a pretty pink cloud, I write: *poetry*. And I affirm *poetry – individual creation*. I explain what *drama* is, what *pathos* is, and I add: these are *eternal values* that in all times will relight the flame in the hearts of men.

This statement, and the accompanying drawing, is perhaps the most eloquent statement made by Le Corbusier of his belief in the poetic potential of technique in architecture. He went on to say,

I shall no longer speak to you of poetry or lyricism. I shall draw precise reasonable things ... I shall talk 'technique' and you, you will react, 'poetry'. And I promise you a dazzling poem: the poem of the architecture of modern times.

The remainder of the lecture is a re-enunciation and elaboration of the arguments of the *cinque points*. The claim that Le Corbusier is making is that, through the adoption of new techniques, architecture will undergo a fundamental transformation, which will invest it with new powers, the creation of a new *poetic*.

By juxtaposing the writings of Geoffrey Scott and Le Corbusier – on the face of it an unlikely pairing – I am trying to establish that it is possible to argue coherently for alternative views of the status of technique in the conception and production of works of architecture. On the one hand is Scott's belief that the essential nature of architecture resides in its humanistic value, as this was expressed in the Renaissance, and that the *mechanical* preoccupations of the Gothic, devotion to the expression of construction as a primary force, are a distraction from this. By contrast, Le Corbusier regards technique, and its expression, as fundamental to the creation of a new language and poetry. In this we may recognise a parallel with the arguments of Ruskin and his devotees in the 'Free School' and, in particular, in its manifestation in the architecture of the Arts and Crafts Movement. And this, of course, conforms to Pevsner's analysis in *Pioneers of Modern Design*,[8] in which the material themes of the Modern Movement are claimed to have their roots in the Arts and Crafts.

All polarities of this kind seem to demand that we should make a decisive choice between them. In principle, I am certain that architectural design must rest on a coherent and consistent view of these questions, pragmatism is the enemy of substance. But this is not to suggest that it is any easy matter to choose between such alternatives.

One of the arguments in support of explicitly expressing construction – *technique* – is that is provides an *objective* basis for the appearance of a building. It thus avoids caprice or fancy and is, therefore, in some way substantial and has value. Stated simplistically, this is in many respects a curious argument, because it denies that a building may have value or purpose other than the mechanical satisfaction of material ends, that architecture is incapable of expressing anything. It is here that Le Corbusier's connection of *technique* with *poetry* becomes apparent. He is *not* saying that the literal observance of technical demands will lead to a poetic architecture. He *is* saying that the new techniques open up the possibility of a new poetic *if* they are invested and applied with imagination. In the Buenos Aires lecture he spoke of the potential of the concrete frame – the *Dom-ino*.

> [O]n a horizontal slab of concrete, on top of pilotis descending to their foundations, I raise the limpid and pure prisms of utilitarian buildings: I am moved by a high intention, I proportion the prisms and the spaces around them; I compose in the atmosphere. Everything counts: the herds, the grass, the flowers in the foreground on which one walks caressing them with one's eyes, the lake, the Alps, the sky ... and the divine proportions.[9]

This statement, incidentally, strikes me as an uncanny premonition of his design for the Convent of La Tourette.

Technique and representation

In their different ways, the arguments of Scott and Le Corbusier oppose the notion that architecture may be based only upon the literal satisfaction of the mechanical elements of construction. This seems to me to be a point of fundamental importance and its corollary, I would argue, is that questions of *technique* are, or should be, at the very centre of architectural theory.

This is precisely the subject of Kenneth Frampton's *Studies in Tectonic Culture: The Poetics of Construction in Nineteenth and Twentieth Century Architecture*,[10] in which he writes,

> Without wishing to deny the volumetric character of architectural form, this study seeks to mediate and enrich the priority given to space by a reconsideration of the constructional and structural modes by which, of necessity, it has to be achieved. Needless to say, I am not alluding to the mere revelation of constructional technique but rather to its expressive potential inasmuch as the tectonic amounts to a poetics of construction

it is art, but in this respect the artistic dimension is neither figurative or abstract.

As I have hinted above, the discussion of the relation of technique to expression should not be limited only to the *structural* and *constructional* aspects of building technique. The enormous growth of the environmental aspects of architecture since the nineteenth century that was first registered in architectural history by Reyner Banham in *The Architecture of the Well-tempered Environment*,[11] places questions of environment and building services firmly in the repertoire of building technique. In the later decades of the twentieth century, a further dimension to the environmental in architecture has emerged with the agenda of sustainability, which has given new focus to the field.

The primary question is of the significance that is placed upon technique in the conception and realisation of a work of architecture. Possible answers may be proposed on an axis that has, at one pole, a position of extreme technical determinism, where everything that is fundamental to a building derives from the definition and resolution of its technical requirements, and, at the other pole, an extreme variant of Geoffrey Scott's argument that architecture is fundamentally a matter of taste and that questions of technique are, at best, secondary concerns of architects or, perhaps, should be delegated to technicians.

These may be caricatures, but views not far from either are not uncommon. For example, there is a particularly deterministic strand of the 'environmental school' that sees strict observance of the goal of sustainability as carrying a moral force that overrides all other considerations. In contrast, in the brief phase of architectural 'post-modernism' there was, for some, a preoccupation with the scenographic that denied any authority of technique. I suggest that there is a position in the middle ground between the two poles that is intellectually coherent in answering the question. This has its basis in the proposition that questions of technique, in the broad definition given above, invest architecture with a necessary degree of objectivity and rigour, but that they are themselves deeply conditioned by cultural and aesthetic judgements. To illustrate the point, I use comparative 'case studies' of significant buildings from the latter years of the twentieth century.

In an essay first published in 1986, I made a comparison between two buildings conceived for the display of works of art: Piano and Rogers' Centre Pompidou (Figure 9.2) and Louis Kahn's Yale Center for British Art at New Haven (Figure 7.5).[12] That study concentrated on the environmental characteristics of the two buildings. Here I extend the discussion to include questions of structure and construction – the complete repertoire of technique.

In their statements of intentions, the architects of both buildings voiced the clear difference in their respective positions. Kahn was always explicitly concerned with the conception of architecture as a manifestation of culture

Figure 9.2 Piano and Rogers, Centre Pompidou. (Emmanuel Thirard/RIBA
        Collections)

and, in my view, most eloquently summarised his position in his sketch of
'Architecture comes from the making of a room'. (Figure 7.1) Here the poetics of space and light are beautifully and succinctly expressed. Piano stated
his and Rogers' approach to Pompidou in entirely different terms:

> There is the relish for the polemical, the provocative, the sending up of
> the accepted idea of a museum and what it is meant to be. At the start
> of the '70s we were at a crossroads, we had to choose between two
> different concepts of culture; either institutional, esoteric, intimidating,
> or something unofficial open and accessible to the general public. We
> opted for the later. ... The building is a diagram. People read it in a
> flash, its 'viscera' are on the outside, you see it all, understand the way
> people get around it, its lifts and escalators.[13]

In comparison, Kahn's drawing reaches back into the 'sombre and archaic'
sources of architecture – in Vincent Scully's memorable phrase.[14] Piano and
Rogers' intention is to challenge the very convention of the museum as institution and, in particular, its representation in architectural language. To
achieve this they choose the structure, material and environmental machin-
ery of the building – its technology. These distinct cultural objectives circum-
scribe and define all the decisions that are made about structure, material
and the nature of the environment in each design. At face value they are

completely different, but a close analysis shows that they share much common ground of technique. Both buildings have framed structures, their enclosures are of pre-fabricated infill panels, and they are both fully air-conditioned. Of particular importance to my argument is the fact that both buildings are absolutely explicit about this. Their essential differences derive, therefore, from the different aesthetic and cultural standpoints of their architects.

A third building, also an art museum, allows me to develop the point further. Robert Venturi's Sainsbury Wing at the National Gallery in London (Figure 9.3) is, in many ways, a critique of Kahn's museum designs. Venturi was critical of Kahn's museums, in particular the Kimbell Art Museum at Fort Worth (Figure 8.8), because he felt that it is not possible to tell whether the light is natural or artificial. In *Learning from Las Vegas*, Venturi and Scott Brown had argued for the authority of historically derived type in the production of works of architecture on the grounds that the Modern Movement '(excluded) a body of traditional practice for the sake of "science"'.[15] They also argued that, in what they term 'orthodox modern architecture', 'the symbolism ... is usually technological and functional, but when these functional elements work symbolically, they do not work functionally'.

Figure 9.3 Robert Venturi, Sainsbury Wing, National Gallery, London. (Janet Hall/ RIBA Collections)

Working from this theoretical position, Venturi produced a building that, while it is certainly a demonstration of *complexity and tradition*, comes very close, in my view, to the boundary of the proprieties of technique by virtue of its devotion to illusion and the deliberate misrepresentation of its essential technical nature. Because of the installation of a complex technical system of shading devices and artificial lighting high in the roof structure, the apparently daylit galleries are only occasionally so – and the pictures themselves are always viewed under artificial light. The appearance of traditional load-bearing masonry is a thin veneer that clads a pragmatic steel frame. The 'substantial' internal walls between the galleries, with their elegant *pietra serena* architraves and skirtings, are plasterboard upon lightweight steel stud frames, forming voids that contain the air-conditioning ducts. When scenography becomes this more important than tectonics – when appearances and the making of a building become so disassociated – I believe that the very nature and definition of architecture are at risk.[16]

In my judgement, this problem is completely avoided in the work of Carlo Scarpa. His two major projects for art museums, the Castelvecchio Museum at Verona (Figure 9.4) and the Gipsoteca Canoviano at Possagno (Figure 7.4), provide convincing evidence of the capability of twentieth-century architecture to apply building techniques that are entirely of their time and

Figure 9.4 Carlo Scarpa, Castelvecchio Museum, Verona. (Dean Hawkes)

a contemporary approach to the internal environment to the production of buildings of the greatest poetry.

The intervention at Castelvecchio carefully differentiates between new construction and ancient fabric through material, form and detail. The open loggia containing the pivotal Cangrande equestrian sculpture is perhaps the most compelling demonstration of this. Scarpa was also a master in the manipulation of natural light in the display of works of art. The relationship of individual works to light sources at Castelvecchio is precisely calculated to reveal their individual qualities, and at Possagno, his invention of the corner windows, two convex and two concave, in the principal cubic space creates a unique and magical effect.[17]

Conclusion

Through the examples I am trying to demonstrate two key points. First, that decisions about technique in architecture are primarily *cultural* and *aesthetic* matters. That it is impossible to base these complex choices solely upon objective, technical considerations. The second point is that architecture of substance always exhibits a clear relationship between technique and expression – that material, structure, construction and environment are essential elements of the expressive language of architecture and that it is at its most eloquent when these are deployed with imagination.

Turning now to questions of education, I am arguing against the division of the discipline into distinct components of *art* and *science*, or of *architecture* and *building*. This all too easily leads to the relegation of technical teaching to a secondary position in the curriculum. It also threatens the integrity of the design studio, where the omission of these fundamental matters from the discourse risks trivialising the basis of designs. The solution is to recognise that architecture is, of necessity, a unified discipline that, while it clearly participates in and refers to the worlds of both art and science, must be primarily understood as a unique enterprise in which these worlds find a unique synthesis that transcends their differences.

In terms of curriculum, I am suggesting that the question of *technique* or *tectonics* (provided the definition of the latter is extended to include the environmental alongside structure and construction) should have a place in courses in the history and theory of architecture. There is now a substantial and growing literature that informs this.[18] The other consequence of the argument is that technical courses should themselves embrace a sense of history and of the relation of technique to theory. This is not to propose a 'softening' of the necessarily objective and quantitative content of structures, construction and environment courses but to urge that they should always be connected to the wider discourses of history and theory to demonstrate their relevance to the design-centred preoccupations of our students.

Notes

1 This essay is based on a paper given at the Building Centre Trust Annual Conference of Teachers of Technology in the Built Environment, held at the University of Warwick, September 1996. An earlier version was published in *The Journal of Architecture*, Volume 1, No. 4, Winter 1996, pp. 335–346.

2 Francis Bacon, cited in Victoria Walsh, 'Real Imagination Is Technical Imagination', in Matthew Gale and Chris Stephens (Eds.), *Francis Bacon*, exhibition catalogue, London, Tate Publishing, 2008.

3 This is interesting in view of Francis Bacon's apparently happy use of both terms.

4 Geoffrey Scott, *The Architecture of Humanism*, London, Constable & Co., 1914.

5 Robert Macleod, *Style and Society: Architectural Ideology in Britain 1835–1914*, London, RIBA Publications, 1971.

6 *L'Esprit Nouveau* was founded in 1920 by Le Corbusier in collaboration with the painter Amédée Ozenfant and the poet Paul Dermée.

7 Le Corbusier, *Precisions: On the Present State of Architecture and City Planning*, Paris, Cres et Cie, 1930. English translation, Cambridge, MA, MIT Press, 1991.

8 Nikolaus Pevsner, *Pioneers of Modern Design: From William Morris to Walter Gropius*, first published as, *Pioneers of the Modern Movement*, London, Faber & Faber, 1936, revised edition, Harmondsworth, Penguin Books, 1960.

9 Le Corbusier, 1930, op cit.

10 Kenneth Frampton, *Studies in Tectonic Culture: The Poetics of Construction in Nineteenth and Twentieth Architecture*, Cambridge, MA, MIT Press, 1995.

11 Reyner Banham, *The Architecture of the Well-Tempered Environment*, London, The Architectural Press, 1969. Second revised edition, Chicago, IL, University of Chicago Press, 1984.

12 Dean Hawkes, 'Space for Services: The Architectural Dimension', in Dean Hawkes, *The Environmental Tradition: Studies in the Architecture of Environment*, London, E. & F.N. Spon, 1995.

13 Renzo Piano quoted in M. Dini, *Renzo Piano: Projects and Buildings 1964–1983*, London, Electa/The Architectural Press, 1985.

14 Vincent Scully, 'Somber and Archaic: Expressive Tension', *Yale Daily News*, 6 November 1953.

15 Robert Venturi, Denise Scott Brown and Steven Izenour, *Learning from Las Vegas*, Cambridge, MA, MIT Press, 1972.

16 See Dean Hawkes, 'The Sainsbury Wing, National Gallery, London', *The Architects' Journal*, August 1991, reprinted in *The Environmental Tradition: Studies in the Architecture of Environment*, op cit, for an extended critique of this building.

17 For an extended discussion of the environmental aspects of Scarpa's works see, Dean Hawkes, 'I Wish I Could Frame the Blue of the Sky', in Dean Hawkes, *The Environmental Imagination: Technics and Poetics of the Architectural Environment*, 2nd Edition, London, Routledge, 2019. For the most comprehensive description of Castelvecchio see, Richard Murphy, *Carlo Scarpa and the Castelvecchio Revisited*, Edinburgh, Breakfast Mission Publishing, 2017.

18 Kenneth Frampton's *Studies in Tectonic Culture*, op cit., and Reyner Banham's *The Architecture of the Well-Tempered Environment*, op cit., are the seminal texts that laid the foundations for a body of further 'cross-disciplinary' scholarship in recent years.

Essay 10[1]
Typology versus invention
Acoustics and the architecture of music performance

Introduction

My first attempt to connect music and acoustics to architecture came with my final design thesis as a student at the Manchester School of Art in the early 1960s. This was a design for an opera house in Edinburgh. In realising this I embarked on a process of self-education to expand the basic acoustics instruction of my architecture school course. My guides were two books: *Acoustics, Noise and Buildings* by P.H. Parkin and H.R. Humphreys, the standard British text of the day, and Leo L. Beranek's *Music, Acoustics and Architecture*, that had recently been published.[2] From these I gained a rudimentary understanding of the fundamentals of acoustics theory and the history and practise of auditorium design. With this I produced a design for my opera house. My proposal for the auditorium was based on the classical Italian 'horseshoe' opera house, which, I learned from Beranek, was 'one of the most stable spaces for music ever designed'. I made detailed hand calculations of the reverberation time of the auditorium at a range of frequencies, using the equations and data I found in Parkin and Humphries, and I made ray-tracing drawings, in plan and cross-section, to describe the direct sound paths and first reflections of sound.

The original version of the present essay was published in 1980 in the *Transactions of the Martin Centre for Architectural and Urban Studies*.[3] There it appeared in conjunction with a group of papers on the acoustics of auditoria and other aspects of auditorium design that derived from a programme of acoustics research, with which I was associated, that had been in progress at the Martin Centre in Cambridge from the early 1970s.[4] My intention in the essay was to place the research in a wider context by exploring the relationship between precedent and the predictive potential of acoustic science theory in making the fundamental decision regarding the form of a music space. This question itself owed a debt to the work that a number of us at the Martin Centre were pursuing at that time in relation to the works of the design theory school by figures such as Christopher Alexander. In particular, I was impressed by the argument presented by my friend and colleague Lionel March in his essay, 'The logic of design and the question

DOI: 10.4324/9781003083023-11

of value', in which he proposed a 'model' for design in which precedent, or 'stereotype' in my then terminology, plays a significant role.[5]

I further developed the essay when I was invited to contribute to a meeting in Venice to debate approaches to the reconstruction of the La Fenice opera house, following the destruction of Giannantonio Selva's beautiful building by fire on 29 January 1996. In my contribution I reviewed developments in the theory and practise of auditorium design, in the years since the first version of my essay, to pose the question of the authority of precedent, specifically that of the destroyed, much loved and acoustically successful auditorium of La Fenice, in the light of later developments in both theory and practise.[6] I had in mind buildings such as Alvar Aalto's Finlandia Hall in Helsinki (1971), his opera house at Essen (1988) and Hans Scharoun's radical and acoustically remarkable transformation of the geometry of the concert hall at the Philharmonie in Berlin (1963), designed in collaboration with the acoustician Lothar Cremer. Of particular relevance for the situation in Venice, was Zaha Hadid's – sadly never to be built – project for an opera house at Cardiff Bay (1994–1996), in which the auditorium form seemed to parallel the innovation of the Philharmonie, translated to the specific circumstances of the opera. My purpose in revisiting the theme for a third time is to take the discussion further in the light of the great number of designs for music performance spaces that have been built in the last quarter of a century, in the hope of adding a little to the architectural story of these remarkable building types and to refresh the discussion of the origin of designs – precedent or theory – typology versus invention?

Sound and architectural form

> Voice is a flowing breath of air, perceptible to the hearing by contact. It moves in an endless number of circular rounds ... Hence the ancient architects, following in the footsteps of nature, perfected the descending rows of seats in theatres from their investigations of the ascending voice.[7]

The association of acoustic theory with architectural form has, perhaps, never been so clearly stated as by Vitruvius. The concentric rows of seats of the ancient theatre are a literal representation of the manner in which sound radiates in open space. The form is an analogue of the theory.

One of the central themes in architectural design theory is the question of the origin of forms. The most familiar prescription is, perhaps, the Modern Movement's mechanistic axiom that *form follows function*.[8] There is, however, much evidence that designs for new buildings are founded upon reference to preexisting buildings, either specific instances or, perhaps more substantially, upon more general descriptions of type.[9]

When the theatre came indoors in the Renaissance, the model was, unsurprisingly, the designs of antiquity, modified acoustically by the complete enclosure of the roofed space. The precedent is powerfully present in the amphitheatres of Palladio's Teatro Olimpico at Vicenza (1585) and Scamozzi's theatre at Sabbioneta (1588), also at Aleotti's Teatro Farnese at Parma, completed in 1628, but here the type underwent a significant and deeply influential evolutionary step, with the introduction of a proscenium arch. By the middle of the seventeenth century, the amphitheatre had evolved further, with the designs of Carlo Fontana for the theatre of SS. Giovani e Paolo in Venice (1654) and the Teatro Tor di Nona in Rome (1666–1670).[10] Here are the first instances of the horseshoe auditorium plan that is possibly one of the most persuasive examples of the power of precedent or type as the basis for design in architecture.

Alongside these developments in built evolution, the study of acoustics was a significant element of 'early modern' science. In *Origins in Acoustics*[11] Frederick V. Hunt identifies the Franciscan friar, Marin Marsenne (1588–1648) as one of the pioneers in the use of graphic 'ray-tracing' to illustrate the reflection of sound in enclosed space.[12] He was quickly followed by the polymath Jesuit priest, Athanasius Kircher (1601–1680), who Hunt suggests, in addition to numerous, sometimes fantastical, acoustic inventions, was the first to apply ray-tracing to architectural design in the images presented in his *Phonurgia Nova*[13] in which he illustrated the focusing of sound from the elliptical ceiling of a room.

In the first decades of the eighteenth century, there is evidence that the new 'theories' did not offer sufficient confidence in the minds of architects. Bernardo Antonio Vittone (1704–1770), the great Torinese architect, renowned for his centrally planned churches, observed,

> The architect who wants to design a building or a part of it, such as a Hall, a Church, a Choir, a Theatre or something similar, where you must be able to hear a bright and clear voice, must take care not to work by futile efforts, *but to use his knowledge of the masters*' (My italics).[14]

Later in the century, precedent and theory came together explicitly in the acoustic investigations of Pierre Patte (1723–1814). In *Essai sur l'architecture théâtrale*, published in 1774, Patte developed an 'ideal' auditorium plan that derived directly from the elliptical form of the horseshoe theatre of Benedetto Alfieri's Teatro Regio in Turin.[15] Patte's design for a Model Theatre shows an elliptical auditorium with its acoustic 'logic' represented by 'sound rays' that illustrate the distribution of sound from a point on the stage to a place towards the rear of the auditorium. The method was quickly adopted across Europe in texts by George Saunders (1780) in London and Carl Ferdinand Langhans (1787) in Berlin.[16]

Throughout the eighteenth and nineteenth centuries, theatres on the horseshoe model were built across Europe and, later, in North America and elsewhere, as opera became a universal art.[17] Significant and influential examples are the Teatro Regio at Turin and Teatro alla Scala Milan

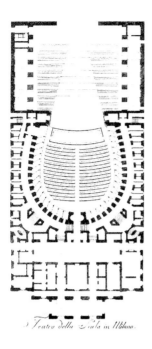

Figure 10.1 Giuseppe Piermarini, Teatro alla Scala, Milan, plan. (Gaetano Mercoli, 1789)

by Giuseppe Piermarini (1778) (Figure 10.1). The reasons for the persistence of the type are numerous, but the question of acoustics is of primary importance. The propagation of sound in an enclosed space depends on a combination of direct and reflected sound, which even in a simple space is analytically a complex process. The emergence of the horseshoe plan was almost certainly the result of a 'Darwinian' process of trial-and-error and, as in natural evolution, unsuccessful variants will have been lost. The form is the expression of the acoustic and, thus, the guarantor of performance. Practise thereby becomes dependent on empirically validated precedent.

A well-documented example of the authority of precedent is found in the case of Charles Garnier's winning entry in the competition for the Paris Opera in 1861. Garnier's experience in determining the design of the auditorium is reported in some detail by Beranek. Garnier made extensive studies of the many acoustic 'theories' of the day, what he referred to as, 'this bizarre science', and discovered, 'A room to have good acoustics must be either long or broad, high or low, of wood or stone, round or square, and so forth'. To find an answer Garnier (1825–1898) turned to precedent, specifically the Grande Theatre de Bordeaux, completed, eighty years earlier in 1780 to the design of Victor Louis (1731–1800), the horseshoe auditorium of which became the model for the Paris building. In summarising his analysis of the acoustics of the opera house, Garnier wrote,

> The European opera house has been the most stable space for music ever designed.
>
> From at least 1700 on, the horseshoe shaped theatre has been built with rings of boxes atop the other and capped by a gallery of low-priced seats. The form has reached its perfection in the Teatro alla Scala which was completed in 1778. The horseshoe design has been copied in nearly every important city in Europe. Ubiquitous is the tiered, circular opera house; thus, composers have been able to write with only one kind of acoustics in mind.[18]

The most significant challenge to the dominance of the horseshoe form came from Richard Wagner. In alliance with Ludwig II of Bavaria and the architect Gottfried Semper, a design for an unexecuted theatre for Munich, 1865–1866, proposed a return to and reinterpretation of the ancient theatre in the form of a single, raked segment of an amphitheatre. This provided the basis for the design and construction of the Festspielhaus in Bayreuth, with the architect, Otto Brückwald, that opened in 1876 (Figure 10.2). This, with Wagner's

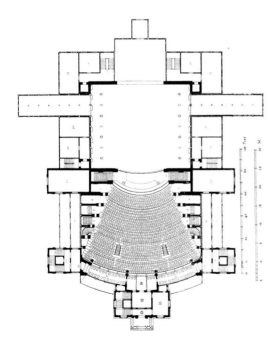

Figure 10.2 Otto Brückwald, Festspielhaus, Bayreuth, plan. (Wood & Bagenal)

innovation of the sunken orchestra pit with a curved plywood canopy, achieved a transformation of the topography and acoustic of the opera auditorium in the realisation of Wagner's vision of the *Gesamptkunstwerk* in his tetralogy, 'Der Ring des Nibelungen'. In the present context, it is worth noting that, however remarkable Wagner's achievement at Bayreuth, it was a minor event in the evolution of the architecture of the opera space, where the utility and cultural associations of the horseshoe form have survived to the twenty-first century. We should also note that the auditorium at Bayreuth is not formally original, but derives from the theatres of antiquity – once again precedent is in play.

Alongside the history and acoustics of the opera house, it is necessary to examine the parallel history of the concert hall, the other significant music per-formance space in western culture. Public performance of instrumental music, whether orchestral or chamber, was a relatively late development. Forsyth gives a detailed account of the emergence of the public concert as a public event in eighteenth-century London, from where concert going spread to the continent of Europe. The first performances took place in existing buildings, such as tav-erns and theatres, but the purpose-designed music space quickly emerged, with the Holywell Music Room in Oxford opening in 1748 and St. Cecilia's Hall in Edinburgh of 1762, leading the way.[19] In London the Hanover Square Rooms opened in 1775 and was the city's principal concert hall for the next 100 years. This was where Joseph Haydn's celebrated London concerts took place. All these spaces were rectangular in plan, a 'shoebox', a type that quickly acquired the utility for the concert music that was enjoyed by the horseshoe in opera. In the nineteenth century, concert halls on this model were built in the major British cities, Exeter Hall, London, built 1831 and enlarged 1850, The Music Hall in Edinburgh, 1845, Philharmonic Hall, Liverpool, 1849, described by the orchestral conductor, Hans Richter, as 'the finest concert hall in Europe'. Manchester followed in 1856 with the Free Trade Hall. The great public halls of the second part of the century, Goldener Saal of the Musikverein, Vienna, 1870, Neues Gewandhaus, Leipzig, 1886, Concertgebouw, Amsterdam, 1888, and just into the new century, Symphony Hall, Boston, 1900 (Figure 10.3), are all variants of the shoebox form with one, or occasionally, two shallow balconies.

At the end of the nineteenth century, in the distinct, but interrelated ques-tion of the design of opera houses and concert halls, the central question of successful acoustic design was resolved at its most fundamental level, the selection of form, by reference to precedent, with the horseshoe dominating for opera and the shoebox for concert music.

The birth of modern architectural acoustics

It was into this situation that W.C. Sabine stepped at the turn of the century, when his series of papers, 'Reverberation' were published in 1900.[20] Sabine was a young professor of physics at Harvard University who, in 1895, was requested by the president of the university, 'to propose changes for remedying

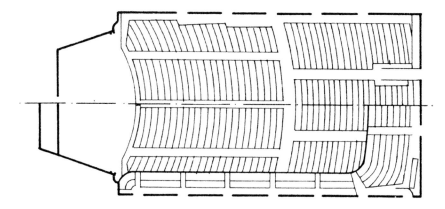

Figure 10.3 McKim, Mead and White, Symphony Hall, Boston, plan. (Dean Hawkes)

the acoustical difficulties in the lecture room of the Fogg Art Museum'.[21] His papers established, for the first time, precise and reliable correlations between the form – albeit primitively defined – and the material of an enclosed space and a measure of its acoustic quality. Sabine made two statements regarding the problem of room acoustics that are, particularly in relation to the condition of nineteenth-century 'theory', of startling clarity. The first is concerned with hearing, the second with the relevant variables of a room.

> In order that hearing may be good in any auditorium, it is necessary that the sound should be sufficiently loud; that the simultaneous components of a complex sound maintain their proper relative intensities; and that the successive sounds in rapidly moving articulation, either of speech or of music, should be clear and distinct, free from each other and free from extraneous noises. These three are the necessary, as they are the entirely sufficient conditions for good hearing.
>
> Broadly considered, there are two, and only two, variables in a room, shape, including size, and materials, including furniture.

The most significant outcome of the research described in the paper was the equation that allows the reverberation time (RT) of a space to be calculated. This is the time, in seconds, that it takes a sound to decay by 60 decibels. The equation, in Imperial units, is:

$$RT = \frac{0.049V}{A}$$

Where: RT is the reverberation time in seconds
0.049 is a constant

V is the volume of the room in cubic feet
A is the quantity of absorbent material

Sabine's papers concluded with an account of the application of his research in the design of the new Boston Music Hall, now Symphony Hall, that was under construction at the time to the design of architects McKim, Mead and White. The paper describes how McKim's first design for the hall was for a Greek theatre form, but that this was abandoned after a visit to Europe, where McKim and the orchestra manager, Henry Higginson, consulted 'musical and scientific authorities' and concluded that such a hall would be 'an untried experiment'. The outcome was that the building committee for the project decided to adopt the conventional rectangular form and to follow the general proportions and arrangement of the Leipzig Gewandhaus, thereby seeking the security of precedent.[22]

Against this background, Sabine brought his new-found understanding of the fundamentals of room acoustics. The proposed hall was to have a larger seating capacity than the Leipzig precedent, 2631 seats rather than 1560, and he pointed out that simple enlargement of the model would have been disastrous, no mistake is easier to make than that of copying an auditorium, but in different materials or to a different scale, in the expectation that the result will be the same. His method was to make systematic comparisons between the Gewandhaus, the existing Boston Music Hall, that was to be replaced by the new building and the design for the new hall itself. From these he calculated the reverberation times of all three:

Leipzig Gewandhaus	2.30 seconds
Old Boston Music Hall	2.44 seconds
New Boston Music Hall	2.31 seconds

The inaugural concert was held on 15 October 1900 and critical response to the acoustics was mixed. The critics from *The Boston Herald* and New York's *Evening Post* both declared the acoustics to be successful and Henry Higginson, who had accompanied McKim on his research visit to European halls, wrote to Sabine after hearing Beethoven's Fifth Symphony at a concert shortly after the inauguration, 'I have never heard the music as now. You have proved here that the Science of Acoustics certainly exists in a definite form. You have done a great part of the hall and everyone thanks you'. But the music critic of the *Boston Evening Transcript*, William Foster Apthorpe, wrote in a dissenting review of the same performance that, 'Things that should sound heroic and awakening, seem merely polite and irreproachable'.[23] The judgement of time, however, is that the Boston acoustics are good. In his survey undertaken 60 years after the hall opened, Beranek reported positive opinions from major conductors, including Bruno Walter, Herbert von Karajan and Sir Adrian Boult and quoted the view of a later Boston critic, Rudolph Elie, Jnr., of the Boston *Herald*, who wrote in 1950, 'It is very clear to me now, that Symphony Hall is the most acoustically beautiful hall in the United States'.[24]

The 'new acoustics' and modern architecture

The relation of science and architecture was to acquire new significance in the century that began with the publication of Sabine's seminal paper and the opening of Boston Symphony Hall. These demonstrated the possibility of a synthesis between theory and practise, albeit realised by confirming the authority of precedent in the shoebox plan and clothed in the conventions of the classical language of architecture. In the succeeding decades, the theory of auditorium acoustics advanced as a second generation of acousticians built upon Sabine's foundations, and this was paralleled by the emergence of new ideas on architecture in which new technologies and elements of scientific thinking were applied in the development of a new aesthetic. This was expressed in 1920 by Le Corbusier in the Introduction to the journal *L'Esprit Nouveau*, 'There is a new spirit of construction and synthesis guided by a clear conception'.[25] My aim here is to sketch an outline of these events in relation to the next stage in the evolution of the architecture of the concert hall.

Sabine died in 1919 at the age of 50. He had continued his acoustics research at Harvard following the publication of his pioneering research on 'Reverberation' and expanded its scope to include studies of sound transmission between rooms and groundbreaking developments in the use of photography, using what he named the 'Toeppler-Boys-Foley' method of photographing air disturbances in scale models of auditoria, thereby making sound visible.[26] In these years he laid the foundations for the establishment of acoustics as a respected subject of study in American universities.[27] In addition, his work attracted attention across the Atlantic Ocean. In 1914, Philip Hope Edward Bagenal, a young Dublin-born architect, began a brief, but significant correspondence with Sabine.[28] Bagenal was injured on the Somme during the First World War and returned to England for treatment at the Eastern General Hospital in Cambridge. There he met the distinguished physicist, Alex Wood, who was also familiar with Sabine's work and had recently published a book, *The Physical Basis of Music*.[29] This meeting led to a collaboration in which they undertook experiments in acoustics that resulted in a book proposal with the title, *Planning for Good Acoustics* being accepted for publication by the syndics of the Cambridge University Press in 1917. In the years following the end of the war both men developed their work and collaboration, Bagenal in architectural practise, in education, teaching at the Architectural Association in London and acoustics consultancy, Wood in physics at Cambridge.[30] *Planning for Good Acoustics* was eventually published in 1931.[31]

In France, Gustave Lyon became the leading authority on acoustics in the same years that Bagenal began his career in Britain. The two men could hardly have emerged from more different backgrounds. Lyon studied civil and mining engineering at, respectively, the École Polytechnique and École des Mines in Paris, following which he joined the musical instrument manufacturer Pleyel et Cie, of which he became head in 1887. At Pleyel, Lyon was responsible for the development of new musical instruments, including a 'wind harp' and a 'double piano'. His first venture in architectural acoustics came when he was invited to advise on the renovation of the Salles des Fêtes at the Palais du Trocadéro in Paris.[32] In 1924, Pleyel et Cie commissioned the architect Jacques Marcel Aubertin to design a new concert hall in Paris with Lyon as acoustics consultant. Aubertin was responsible for the general architectural elements of the building, the plan, elevations and detail, but the auditorium was, in a clear division of labour, entirely the responsibility of Lyon. The 3000-seat Salle Pleyel was completed in 1927.[33] As Darò demonstrates,[34] a vital tool of Lyon's acoustics work was his development of geometric representation of the reflection of sound in a space. The method was applied in the project to modify the acoustics at the Palais du Trocadéro and played a central part in the development of the auditorium at the Salle Pleyel. This hall occupies a crucial place in the evolution of the form of the concert hall by being the first built example of the 'directed sound' auditorium.[35] This adopts the 'fan-shape' plan and the cross-section has an acoustically generated parabolic profile, in all respects a significant departure from the 'shoebox'. At Salle Pleyel the 'modernity' of the auditorium, in form and material, was in contrast to the restrained neo-classicism of Aubertin's architecture for the façade and the foyers, through which the audience passed *en route* to the auditorium from the rue du Faubourg Saint-Honoré.

A link between Gustave Lyon and his English contemporaries, Bagenal and Wood is made explicit in *Planning for Good Acoustics*. In a discussion of, 'Development of simple auditory type', Bagenal and Wood wrote,

> If we develop logically the principle of the useful reflecting surface we reach two main types of plan, namely (i) the fan-shaped, (ii) the paraboloid. Of these (i) the fan-shaped is the simpler and more generally useful for all types of auditories. *Much failure and inconvenience would be avoided in acoustics if the fan-shape could be used in preference to square or oblong.* (My italics)

The argument is illustrated with a reference to the Salle Pleyel, illustrated with long and cross-sections and a plan showing the combination of the fan-shaped plan and the parabolic curve of the ceiling showing plotted sound rays. (Figure 10.4) This is described as 'a compromise between the fan and the parabola. The consequent loudness of tone is admitted on all hands'. Here we find the 'new' auditorium form receiving, virtually simultaneously, the sanction of both theory and practise. In their apparent criticism of 'square or oblong' it appears that Bagenal and Wood are rejecting the authority of precedent as their theoretical studies move on from Sabine's support for the shoebox.

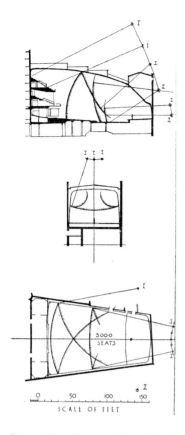

Figure 10.4 Jacques Marcel Aubertin with Gustave Lyon, Salle Pleyel, Paris, plan
and sections. (Wood & Bagenal)

The link between acoustic science and modern architecture was formed
when Gustave Lyon collaborated with Le Corbusier and Pierre Jeanneret in
their competition entry for the Palace of the League of Nations at Geneva
launched in 1926. The assembly hall, to accommodate 2675 people, was
a space for speech – not music – but the form is closely related to the
Salle Pleyel auditorium (Figure 10.5). It is recorded that Lyon visited Le
Corbusier's atelier at 35 rue de Sèvres to discuss the project as the design
developed.[36] The acoustic principles behind the design of the assembly hall
were explicitly illustrated in the competition entry with drawings showing
the reflections of sound waves in plan and cross-section, an illustration of
Lyon's geometrical approach that closely resembles Bagenal and Wood's
analytical diagrams. The acoustic collaboration between Le Corbusier and
Lyon continued in 1931 with the unbuilt project for the Palace of the Soviets
in Moscow. Here the assembly hall takes the characteristic 'fan' form, now
for an audience of 6500. Neither of these projects was built, so the effectiveness of the designs remains, alas, untested.

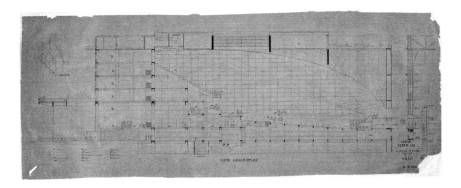

Figure 10.5 Le Corbusier and Pierre Jeanneret with Gustave Lyon, Palace of the
League of Nations, auditorium section. (FLC/ADAGP, Paris and DACS,
London 2021)

The emergence of the fan-shaped concert hall in the first decades of the
twentieth century raises an important question in the argument on the relation of precedent and theory. In contrast to Sabine's role in the design of the
Boston New Music Hall, where he applied science to validate an auditorium
form explicitly derived from precedent, the auditorium at Salle Pleyel was
generated in its most fundamental form and material from theoretical principles. I suggest that this became possible following from Sabine's founding
research and the subsequent development that was taken on by Lyon and
his British contemporaries, Bagenal and Wood. But, in the wider context
of my exploration of precedent and theory, it is interesting to observe how,
in the years following the opening of the Salle Pleyel and Le Corbusier's
engagement with Lyon in the projects for the League of Nations and the
Palace of the Soviets, the fan-shaped auditorium was quickly replicated in
the design of halls around the world. The two earliest examples were the
Philharmonic Hall in Liverpool, United Kingdom, to the design of architect
Herbert J. Rowse, 1939, and the Kleinhans Music Hall in Buffalo, USA,
1940, by the Finnish-American architect, Eliel Saarinen. The Philharmonic
Hall seats an audience of 2755 in an auditorium that has been described as
'art-deco' in style. Nikolaus Pevsner described the exterior of the building
as in the 'Dutch-Dudok style'[37] and the building was very much an expression of its time.[38] The Kleinhans Hall has 2839 seats and is, architecturally,
emphatically of the twentieth century, with the walls lined with elegantly
detailed primavera wood panels.

These halls and their numerous successors[39] provoke the question of origins of the form. Is this the outcome of a 'logical' process in which theoretical principles of the physics of sound are translated into architectural form?
Or, in these 'second generation' examples, is the precedent of the fan-shaped
Salle Pleyel the primary influence of the design? Theory or precedent?

The return of the 'shoebox'

The Royal Festival Hall in London was one of the first major concert halls to be built following the end of the Second World War (Figure 10.6). It was designed between 1948 and 1951 by a team led by Leslie Martin at the London County Council. Hope Bagenal led the acoustics team assisted by Peter Parkin and William Allen of the Building Research Establishment.[40] At its completion, the building was described as, 'the first modern building in Britain to be designed within the orbit of modern architectural ideas'.[41] The collaboration between architectural design and acoustic science was both a practical necessity and a symbol of modernity. The hall was to accommodate an audience of around 3000, much larger than those of the majority of existing examples. In reviewing the acoustic design in 1953, two years after the hall was opened, Parkin, Allen, Purkis and Scholes, the team from the Building Research Station, acknowledged Bagenal's 'long and varied experience' when defining the musical requirements as '(i) definition, (ii) fulness of tone, (iii) balance, (iv) blend, (v) no echoes, and (vi) a low level of intruding noise. In addition, it was thought important to obtain reasonably uniform acoustics over the whole audience area'.[42]

The question of the plan form of the hall was, of course, fundamental. Bagenal discussed the matter at length in a paper published in the year the hall was completed,

> Another principle accepted was the rectangular plan in preference to the fan, because it permits of more inter-reflections, hence longer

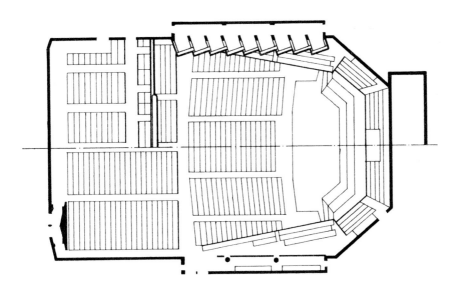

Figure 10.6 London County Council Architect's Department, Royal Festival Hall, London, plan. (Dean Hawkes)

reverberation in a crowded hall, and does not ask aesthetically for the dangerous plan curves to seat rows, parapets, rear walls, which tend to bring sound back to a front focal area and do harm in modern designs.[43]

Here we have Bagenal rejecting the assertion giving strong support to the fan-shaped hall, which he and Wood made in *Design for Good Acoustics* just two decades earlier.[44] Barron concisely summarised the process:

> The consultants … weighed the fan shape against the traditional rectangular plan form and decided to use the rectangular plan, bearing in mind its good, unchallenged reputation.[45]

The precedent was, however, modified in a number of ways. Barron observes that, 'For a hall the size of the Festival Hall with 2900 seats, it is not possible simply to scale up the classical design'.[46] To accommodate the audience within acceptable distance from the stage, the width of the hall is 32 metres, so, to bring the stage to an acceptable dimension for an orchestra, the side walls are splayed. In addition, the traditional side balconies are replaced by groups of boxes on the side walls. In cross section the flat floor of precedent is replaced by a low-angle rake with additional seating in a Grand Tier and the ceiling is profiled to enhance early reflections, again in contrast to the flat, coffered ceilings of the shoebox. Barron succinctly summarises, 'If its plan can be seen as a development of the classical rectangular plan, in its long section the Festival Hall owes some debt to the experiments of previous decades'.[47] Precedent is here transformed in a kind of architectural Darwinism as one 'species' overlaps the other.

In my discussion of this theme that was referenced by Lionel March in his essay, 'The logic of design and the question of value',[48] I outlined 'An evolutionary tale' in which I suggested that, in relation to the design of a specific building type (in that instance the office building) 'there is, at any point of time, a generally held notion about the nature of a good solution … and it is that notion which frequently informs the initial design hypothesis'.[49] In that essay I used the term *stereotype* to identify the 'generally held notion', that is the equivalent of the use here of *precedent*. The later work on the value of precedent in the design of auditoria was further validation of this argument, which was reinforced by the evidence of the durability of the precedents of the horseshoe opera theatre and the shoebox concert hall. These were longer-lived than the distinct stereotypes for the office building, as that had evolved from the nineteenth and through the twentieth century, under the pressures of, 'changing building technology, organisational ideas and physical, social and cultural environments'. The shift from the shoebox to the fan-shape is an illustration of a similar process at play in auditorium design, with a new precedent or stereotype challenging the long-held authority of the other. The case of the Royal Festival Hall may be seen to be a further instance of this evolutionary process and itself became a powerful precedent for a number of subsequent halls.[50]

The 'other' tradition

The evolutionary tradition of concert hall design was challenged in the post-war years by the work of two of the great architects of the time, Alvar Aalto in Finland and Hans Scharoun in Germany.[51] They are amongst those whom Colin St John Wilson identified as members of 'the other tradition of modern architecture'.[52] The essence of this is expressed by Aalto in his essay, 'The Humanising of Architecture' in which he wrote, 'To make architecture more human means better architecture, and it means a functionalism much larger than the merely technical one'.[53] Throughout Aalto's work, we find a concern for the environments of buildings.[54] In describing his design for the North Jutland Art Museum at Aalborg in Denmark, he drew an explicit analogy between light and sound, when he stated, 'Light has the same significance for an art museum as acoustics for a concert hall'.[55] This link is expressed in the numerous design drawings in which he explores properties of heat, light and, our concern here, sound. At the Viipuri Library, completed in 1935, we have sketches that show the distribution and inter-reflection of both natural and artificial light and the distribution of warmth in the reading room and a ray-trace diagram of the distribution of sound in the lecture hall. Similar sketches exist for all the major projects, and acoustics diagrams are central to the conception of the sequence of auditorium projects that he designed.[56] The projects for the unbuilt Kuopio Theatre competition, 1952, and the realised designs for Kultuuritalo, 1955–1958, the Finlandia Hall, 1962–1971 (Figure 10.7), both in Helsinki, and the Opera House at Essen, 1959–1964 (Figure 10.8) illustrate his individual interpretation of

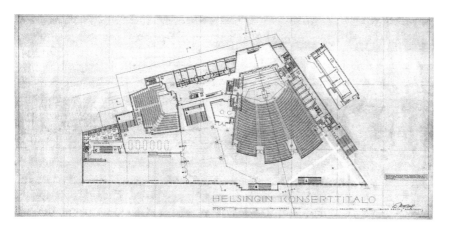

Figure 10.7 Alvar Aalto, Finlandia Hall, Helsinki, plan. (Aalto Foundation)

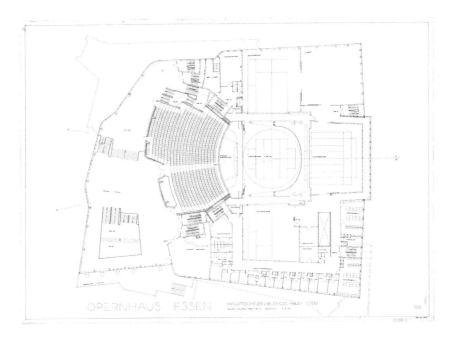

Figure 10.8 Alvar Aalto, Opera House, Essen, plan. (Aalto Foundation)

the nature of spaces for music performance. In these projects the auditorium is a development of the fan-shape precedent, becoming asymmetrical and informal in comparison with the strict symmetry of conventional halls. The acoustic performance of these spaces was variable. Kultuuritalo, being highly regarded, but Finlandia less so.[57] Essen, which was completed in 1998 twelve years after Aalto's death, is a synthesis of the asymmetrical fan form with a reinterpretation of the tiered boxes of the classical opera house and is highly regarded.

Hans Scharoun's design for the Philharmonie concert hall in Berlin, 1956–1963, took the spatial informality of Aalto's designs to a new level, which was principally a matter of plan form, with the invention of the 'vineyard' form (Figure 10.9). The story of the conception and development of the design, with emphasis on the interaction between the architect and his acoustic consultant, Lothar Cremer, is well-documented.[58] Scharoun wrote, 'Music as the focal point; this was the keynote from very beginning. This dominating thought not only gave shape to the auditorium ... but also ensured its undisputed priority within the entire building scheme'. He continued with the observation that, 'Can it be an accident that whenever improvised music is heard, people tend to gather around the performers in a circle? The psychological basis of this natural process seems self-evident; it had only to be transposed into a concert hall'.[59]

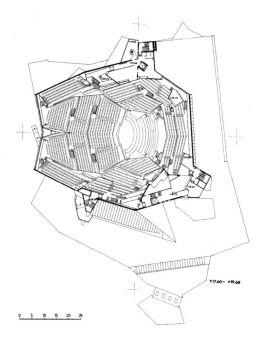

Figure 10.9 Hans Scharoun, Philharmonie, Berlin, plan. (Akademie der Künste, Berlin, Hans Scharoun Archive)

This statement was a challenge, in the light of the history of the concert hall, but Cremer entered into a remarkable collaboration with Scharoun and the principal conductor of the Berlin Philharmonic Orchestra, Herbert von Karajan. The form that emerged, in which the distribution of early reflections of sound is promoted by the vertical planes of the vineyard terraces of the seating, was a striking innovation in both plan and cross-section. The terraces, in response to Scharoun's reference to improvised performance, are disposed around the orchestra, with the conductor's podium close to the centre of the space. In plan the hall is symmetrical, with just the organ placed off-axis to the right of the platform. In cross-section, the convex curves of the tent-like ceiling help to diffuse the sound. In use the hall has been judged to be a success, in Barron's summary, 'as a concert experience the Philharmonie is indeed remarkable'.[60]

The Philharmonie Legacy

In the evolutionary history of the concert hall, the Philharmonie is significant because it is arguably the first instance in which the science of acoustics, in the lineage from the pioneer, Sabine, through the generation of Bagenal and Lyon, and on to the consolidation of both science and profession in the post-war years, working in collaboration with an architect of the greatest insight and intuition, led to the invention of a new form of hall. Theory had overtaken precedent. The building has influenced numerous progeny in the half-century since it was completed. One of the first was the St David's Hall in Cardiff, architect J. Seymour Harris with acoustics consultant Sandy Brown, opened in 1982. Barron wrote that this hall, with its vineyard plan, 'owes an obvious debt to Scharoun's masterpiece, though lacks some of the subtlety of its predecessor'.[61] This was soon followed by Suntory Hall in Tokyo which opened in 1986. The architects were Yasui Architects, but in the present discussion, the contribution of the acoustics consultant, Yasuhisa Toyota, of Nagata Acoustics, Tokyo, is much more significant. The 2006-seat main auditorium is a vineyard on the model of the Philharmonie and has received a positive critical response, including from von Karajan. Toyota has gone on to work on new vineyard halls across the world, often in collaboration with prominent architects. In chronological order of their opening dates these include:

Sapporo Concert Hall 'Kitura', 1997. Architect: Hokkaido Engineering
Walt Disney Concert Hall, Los Angeles, 2003. Architect: Frank Gehry
DR Konserthuset, Copenhagen, 2009. Architect: Jean Nouvel
Helsinki Music Centre, 2011. Architect: Laitio-Pullinen-Raurio
Elbphilharmonie, Hamburg, 2017. Architect: Herzog and de Meuron.

To these we should add Jean Nouvel's Philharmonie de Paris, which opened in 2015 (Figure 10.10). This is described as a 'surround-type'. Here there was a comprehensive team of acoustic advisors. For the architectural competition that led to the appointment of Nouvel, the clients

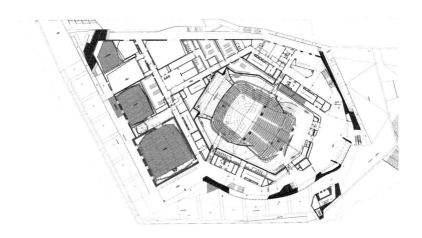

Figure 10.10 Jean Nouvel, Philharmonie de Paris, plan. (Jean Nouvel)

appointed acousticians Echard Kahle and Richard Denayrou to prepare the 'Programme Acoustique', a 40-page document. Nouvel engaged the New Zealand acousticians, Marshall Day at the competition stage and they remained consultants for the realisation of the building. Finally, Yasu Toyota served as 'peer review' in an advisory role.[62] Marshall and Day described the specific design as, 'two nested chambers – an inner space producing visual and acoustical intimacy between audience and performer – and an outer space with its own architectural and acoustical presence providing the high reverberance required by the brief'. This idea, that first emerged in a sketch made at a breakfast meeting, may be seen as a further evolutionary step of Scharoun and Cremer's original design for the Philharmonie.[63]

Pluralism

It is notable that there was an interval of two decades between the completion of the Philharmonie and the emergence of the vineyard form as a widely copied precedent for the design of concert halls. But the recent proliferation of the type provides strong support for the proposition that precedent continues to be a powerful influence in the design of complex buildings, even as theoretical understanding of the fundamentals of acoustics has expanded far beyond the foundations established by Sabine over a century ago.

The tools of acoustic analysis have evolved considerably in the twentieth century, with significant advances, first, in the use of scale models of auditoria in which to carry out both objective and subjective assessment of designs. These have been followed and, in some instances, supplemented by the development of computer simulation tools that have played a major part in the design development of many recent halls. An authoritative review of the evolution of the forms of concert halls from the mid-nineteenth century to the end of the twentieth has been constructed by Barron.[64] In this a clear typology of auditorium form is given: shoebox, theatre form, fan-shape, terraced, other (oval, hexagon, surround, in-the-round).[65] The analysis clearly shows the emergence of vineyard halls following the opening of the Philharmonie, but also shows the persistence of shoebox form and a number of halls that fall into the 'other' category, although here, as Barron's definition shows, there are a number of possible forms. Barron nicely describes these halls, which were built from the 1970s, as 'eclectic'. He lists Christchurch, New Zealand (1972) – *elliptical*; the concert hall of the Sydney Opera House (1973) – *elongated hexagon*; Boetticher Hall, Denver Performing Arts Center (1978) – *surround*; Muziecentrum, Utrecht (1979) – *in-the-round*. At this period, there were important advances in acoustics theory. Barron is, once again, a guide to these, writing, 'By the early 1980s a series of quantities were available to measure and modelling possibilities available to test out designs. *However, translating preferred values of objective measures into a 3-dimensional concert hall design is far from trivial*'

(My italics). One of the significant theoretical developments in this period was the recognition of the importance of early reflections of sound from the side, defined by Marshall as the quality of 'spatial responsiveness'.[66] This was applied in practise by Marshall in his role as acoustics consultant for the Christchurch City Hall in New Zealand.

To conclude this analysis, we will look further into this group and then return to the continuing survival of the shoebox. Barron's analysis included no fewer than 15 'halls derived from the nineteenth-century shoebox halls' constructed between 1971 and 1998, a demonstration of both the continuing validity of this form as the theory of auditorium acoustics has gained ground. The type continues to find favour into the twenty-first century. Three buildings, all of distinctive architectural quality, serve to support the point; the Sibelius Hall, Lahti, Finland, architects Hannu Tika and Kimmo Lintula, opened in 2000; Aarhus Synfonisk Sall, Denmark, architects C.F. Møller, completed in 2008; and Sage Gateshead in the United Kingdom, by Norman Foster, 2004 (Figure 10.11), where a sinuous exterior encloses a strictly orthogonal 1700 seat shoebox hall along with two smaller halls. The designers of the last two of these make specific reference to Vienna's Goldener Saal of the Musikverein as influencing the form and dimensions of their halls.

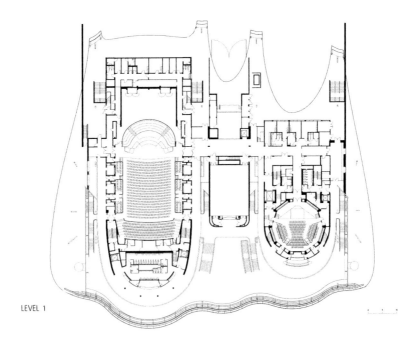

LEVEL 1

Figure 10.11 Norman Foster, The Sage, Gateshead, plan. (Foster Partners)

The 'modern' opera house

As referred to above, Aalto's Essen Opera House, which opened in 1998, shared his innovative approach to the modern auditorium. The asymmetrical fan shape is combined with arrays of boxes that line the side and rear walls in a reinterpretation of the classical model, an evolutionary rather than a revolutionary step, perhaps. The ambitious project for the Opéra Bastille in Paris in 1989 was the outcome of an architectural competition won by Carlos Ott. The 2700 seat auditorium is described as an 'arena' form with two large balconies, quite unlike the traditional model in dimension and form. Its acoustics have not been considered a success. Other opera houses in recent decades have often reverted to the security of tradition with horseshoe auditoria at Glyndebourne in the United Kingdom in 1994, by Michael Hopkins, with Arup Acoustics and at Operahuset in Oslo, which opened in 2008 to the design of Snøhetta, once again working with Arup Acoustics (Figure 10.12). There the horseshoe auditorium is enclosed in an external envelope of striking modernity, quite unrelated to the classical origins of the performance space. In both cases, the expertise of the consultants has been successfully combined with the authority of precedent.

In 1994 an international architectural competition was held for a new house for the Welsh National Opera in Cardiff. The acoustic brief was the work of Derek Sugden of Arup Acoustics.

> The architect and acoustician ... should endeavour to create an acoustic where the geometry is so carefully contrived as to provide reflections to ensure that those parts of the opera which must be intelligible are heard

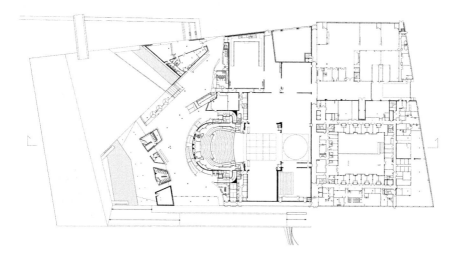

Figure 10.12 Snøhetta, Operahuset, Oslo, plan. (Snøhetta)

against a background which does not reduce the richness and warmth of an orchestral sound and voice, and enhances rather than threatens the drama of the occasion. The theatrical and acoustic qualities of an opera house are wholly interdependent. They should be analogous with or a paradigm of the opera itself: that extraordinary combination of music, poetry, prose and theatre which achieves the pinnacle of European art and creativity when there is a perfect synthesis in its creation and performance.

Moving on to more technical matters the brief stated,

the geometry explicitly described in this brief will give short side reflections and a powerful direct sound ensuring no loss of clarity and speech intelligibility for the classical operas and the reverberant field will provide a warm rich sound that is so necessary for the operas of Verdi and Wagner.[67]

The brief was careful to avoid explicit reference to precedent or form, but it was possible to infer that a horseshoe house would meet the requirements, both poetic and objective.[68] The winning design was submitted by Zaha Hadid and emphatically rejected tradition in either the form of the auditorium or the building as a whole (Figure 10.13). In post-competition

Figure 10.13 Zaha Hadid, Cardiff Bay Opera House, plan. (ZHA)

development, Hadid worked with Arup Acoustics and the auditorium as it developed bore similarities to Aalto's arrangement at Essen, with galleries and boxes hovering above racked stalls. The configuration would appear to meet the requirement for 'short side reflections and a powerful direct sound'.

Conclusion

The modern science of architectural acoustics has developed enormously since Wallace Clement Sabine established its first secure basis at the beginning of the twentieth century. This is particularly so in relation to the design of spaces for music performance in concert halls and opera houses. Particular progress has followed from the adoption of physical models in the 1970s and the introduction of computer simulation methods from the 1980s onwards. In the first modern collaboration between science and architecture in the design of an auditorium, the new Boston Music Hall, science was used to bring a degree of certainty by seeking to replicate an acoustic measure of architectural *precedent*, the reverberation times of the Leipzig Gewandhaus and the old Boston Music Hall, in the new hall. The fundamental question of the *form* of the hall remained a matter of precedent – the rectangular shoebox.

Two decades later the Modern Movement opened up new relationships between acoustics and architecture. In the footsteps of Sabine, architectural acoustics developed further through the work of figures like Bagenal and Wood in Britain and Gustave Lyon in France. The connection of theory and modern architectural practise was established through Lyon's collaborations with Le Corbusier in the unrealized projects for the League of Nations building and the Palace of the Soviets, in which Lyon's 'invention' of the fan-shaped auditorium at the Salle Pleyel became the Modern Movement's symbol of acoustic design. It also received the 'theoretical' approval of Bagenal and Wood and was rapidly adopted as a precedent for numerous halls around the world. The form continued in use in the post-war years, but, in one of the most documented instances of collaboration between architecture and acoustics – the Royal Festival Hall in London, the shoebox, albeit in modified form, was adopted as the basis of the design, with the authority of Bagenal, who was the lead consultant. This important project influenced the design of many other rectangular halls.

Against this background of co-existence between the fan-shape and the shoebox came a period of reinvention. This was led by architects who belonged to the 'Other' tradition of modern architecture, specifically Alvar Aalto in Finland and Hans Scharoun in Germany. Aalto's auditorium designs may be presented as fan-shaped, but, with their asymmetry in plan, they mark an important development in both the social and acoustic nature of these spaces. In my analysis, Aalto's designs foreshadowed the remarkable moment in the history of the concert hall that came with Hans Scharoun's design, with the vital collaboration of the acoustics consultant,

Lothar Cremer, in the design of the Philharmonie in Berlin. The vineyard plan emerged from Scharoun's insight into the physical relationship between performer and audience in which he placed the performance at the centre of the space in contrast to the 'end wall' arrangement of all earlier halls. From this followed Cremer's realisation of the potential of the vineyard surfaces to provide first reflections of sound and thereby transformed the conception of the concert hall. The power of this is demonstrated by the proliferation of halls on this model in the years since the Philharmonie opened in 1963.

In the twenty-first century, the science and art of auditorium acoustics have advanced far from the tentative beginnings made by Sabine in Boston. In this essay, I have attempted to construct an account of the events, scientific and architectural, that have marked these developments. The philosopher of science, P.B. Medawar wrote,

> As a science advances, particular facts are comprehended within, and therefore in a sense annihilated by, general statements of steadily increasing explanatory power and compass – whereupon the facts need no longer be known explicitly, i.e., spelled out and kept in mind. In all sciences we are being progressively relieved of the burden of singular instances, the tyranny of the particular. We need no longer record the fall of every apple.[69]

The science of auditorium acoustics now easily meets Medawar's criterion, and in architecture there exists a rich typography of auditorium forms, precedents, supported by the authority of scientific validation, that have placed this once 'bizarre science' on more substantial foundations.

Notes

1 This essay is a greatly extended version of a paper first published in, Philip Steadman and Janet Owers (Eds.), *Transactions of the Martin Centre for Architectural and Urban Studies*, Department of Architecture, University of Cambridge, Volume 4, 1980, pp. 3–16.
2 P.H. Parkin and H.R. Humphries, *Acoustics, Noise and Building*, 1st Edition, London, Faber & Faber, 1958. Leo L. Beranek, *Music, Acoustics and Architecture*, New York & London, John Wiley & Son, 1962.
3 *Transactions of the Martin Centre for Architectural and Urban Studies*, Volume 4, Cambridge, Woodhead-Faulkner, 1980. In this form, the essay was also published in Dean Hawkes, *The Environmental Tradition: Studies in the Architecture of Environment*, London, E & F.N. Spon, 1996.
4 This work, which was directed by Professor Peter Parkin and supported by the Building Research Station (BRS), 1975–1978, and the Science Research Council (SRC), 1978, used physical models, at a scale of 1:8, to study the acoustics of proposed auditoria. Specific projects were undertaken in connection with the design of the Olivier Theatre at the National Theatre and the concert hall of the Barbican Centre. My role was as the departmental 'investigator' for the project and the research studies were carried out by acousticians Dr. Michael Barron and Dr. Raf Orlowski.

5 Christopher Alexander's, *Notes on the Synthesis of Form*, Cambridge, MA, Harvard University Press, 1967 was a key reference at this time. Lionel March's, 'The Logic of Design and the Question of Value', in Lionel March (Ed.), *The Architecture of Form*, Cambridge, UK, Cambridge University Press, 1976, was a major critique of Alexander's argument.

6 Dean Hawkes, 'Precedent and Theory in the Design of Auditoria: The Case of La Fenice Venezia', in Claudia Canella and Licia Cavasin (Eds.), *La Fenice: Verso La Riconsruzione*, Venice, Fondazione Ugo e Olga Levi, 1996.

7 Vitruvius, *The Ten Books of Architecture*, Book V, Ch. IV.6, (Trans.) W.H. Morgan, New York, Dover Books, 1960.

8 The expression is attributed to the American architect, Louis Sullivan, in an essay, 'The Tall Office Building Artistically Considered', first published in *Lippincott's Magazine* March 1896, reprinted in Tim and Charlotte Benton with Dennis Sharp (Eds.), *Form and Function: A Sourcebook for the History of Architecture and Design 1890–1939*, London, Granada Publishing Ltd., 1975. The exact original quote is 'form ever follows function'.

9 Alan Colquhoun, 'Typology and Design Method', in *Essays in Architectural Criticism*, Cambridge, MA, MIT Press, 1985.

10 See, Michael Forsyth, *Buildings for Music: The Architect, the Musician, and the Listener from the Seventeenth Century to the Present Day*, Cambridge, UK, Cambridge University Press, 1985.

11 Frederick V. Hunt, *Origins in Acoustics: The Science of Sound from Antiquity to the Age of Newton*, New Haven, CT, Yale University Press, 1978.

12 Marin Marsenne, *Traité de l'harmonie universelle*, Paris, 1636–1637.

13 Athanasius Kircher, *Phonurgia Nova*, 1673.

14 Marco Caniato and Vilma Fasoli, 'Bernardo Antonio Vittone: Acoustics and Architecture in the XVII Century', *Proceedings of Meetings on Acoustics*, Acoustical Society of America, Vol. 4, 2008.

15 Michael Forsyth, *Buildings for Music*, op cit.

16 George Saunders, *Treatise on Theatres*, London, The Architectural Library, 1780; Carl Friedrich Langhans, *Ueber Theater*, Berlin, Gottfried Hayn, 1810. An extensive study of the acoustics of German theatres in the Romantic period, with particular emphasis on Langhans, is, Joseph L. Clarke, 'Catacoustic Enchantment: The Romantic Conception of Reverberation', in *Grey Room 60*, Massachusetts Institute of Technology, Summer 2016. A Europe-wide study of the developing relationship between acoustics and theatre design is, Viktoria Tkaczyk, 'Listening in Circles: Spoken Drama and the Architects of Sound, 1750–1839', *Annals of Science*, Vol. 71, Issue 3, 2014, pp. 299–334.

17 Teatro alla Scala, Milan, architect Giuseppe Piermarini, completed in 1778.

18 Charles Garnier, *Le Nouvel Opera de Paris*, Paris, Ducher, 1878, quoted in Leo. L. Beranek, op cit.

19 The Holywell Music Room is the oldest surviving purpose-built concert hall in Europe.

20 The papers first appeared, serially, in *American Architect and Building News*, Vol. 68, from 7 April to 16 June. They were also published in the *Engineering Record* in 1900. They were published in full in, Wallace C. Sabine, *Collected Papers on Acoustics*, Cambridge, MA, Harvard University Press, 1922. Reprinted edition, with Introduction by Frederick V. Hunt, New York, Dover Publications, 1964.

21 Wallace C. Sabine in 'Reverberation' *American Architect and Building News*, op cit.

22 The Leipzig Gewandhaus referred to here was completed in 1886 and was the work of architects Paul Gropius and Heinrich Schmieden. The hall replaced an earlier building built in 1781 and was itself destroyed in a bombing raid in 1944. Its modern replacement opened in 1981.

23 For a comprehensive review of the first responses to the hall, see Emily Thompson, *The Soundscape of Modernity: Architectural Acoustics and the Culture of Listening in America, 1900–1933*, Cambridge, MA, MIT Press, 2002.

24 Leo L. Beranek, *Music, Acoustics and Architecture*, op cit.

25 Le Corbusier, Programme of *L'Esprit Nouveau*, No. 1, Paris, October 1920.

26 The Toeppler-Boys-Foley method of photographing sound waves in scale models was illustrated in Sabine's paper, 'Theatre Acoustics', first published in *The American Architect*, Vol. 104, 1913. Reprinted in Wallace Clement Sabine, *Collected Papers on Acoustics*, op cit.

27 This period is described in detail by Emily Thompson in *The Soundscape of Modernity*, op cit. Here she reports that, by the 1930s, courses in architectural acoustics were taught at Harvard, MIT, the universities of Illinois, Iowa and Indiana and the University of California at Los Angeles.

28 This correspondence is discussed in Fiona Smyth, 'A Centenary of Architectural Acoustics', *Proceedings of the Institute of Acoustics*, Vol. 36, Pt. 3, 2014.

29 Alex Wood, *The Physical Basis of Music*, Cambridge, UK, Cambridge University Press, 1913.

30 See Fiona Smyth, 'A Centenary of Architectural Acoustics', op cit, for an account of the meeting and collaboration of Bagenal and Wood.

31 Hope Bagenal and Alex Wood, *Designing for Good Acoustics*, London, Methuen & Co., 1931.

32 Carlotta Darò, 'Lines for Listening: On Gustave Lyon's Geometrical Approach to Acoustics', *The Journal of Architecture*, Vol. 23, No. 6, 2018, pp. 881–902.

33 Auburtin died in 1926 and the building was completed by his collaborators André Granet and Jean-Baptiste Mathon. The auditorium was badly damaged by fire on 28 June 1928 and was subsequently renovated with the seating reduced to 2400. The hall served as Paris' main concert venue, with further renovation in 2002–2006, until 2015, when the Philharmonie de Paris, designed by Jean Nouvel, opened at the Parc de la Villette.

34 Carlotta Darò, 'Lines for Listening: On Gustave Lyon's Geometrical Approach to Acoustics', op cit.

35 See Michael Forsyth, *Buildings for Music*, op cit.

36 The project is comprehensively illustrated in Le Corbusier and Pierre Jeanneret, *Oeuvre Complète*, Zurich, Girsberger, 1937. The relationship between the architects and their acoustics consultant is explored in detail in S. von Fischer, 'Listening and the League of Nations: Acoustics Are the Argument', *Le Corbusier, 50 Years Later*, International Congress, Valencia, 2015.

37 Nikolaus Pevsner, *The Buildings of England: South Lancashire*, Harmondsworth, Penguin Books, 1969.

38 Rowse was an architect who practised a variety of architectural styles over his career. It has been recorded that, on receiving the commission for the Philharmonic Hall, he recruited a young graduate of the Liverpool School of Architecture, Alwyn Edward Rice, who had, in 1932, designed a concert hall for his thesis project. The executed design is said to closely resemble the thesis project in its architectural style and in the form of the auditorium. Joseph Sharples (Ed.), *Charles Reilly and the Liverpool School of Architecture 1904–1933*, Liverpool, Liverpool University Press, 1996.

39 Important post-war examples of fan-shaped halls, both completed in 1957, were included by Leo L. Beranek in *Music, Acoustics and Architecture*, op cit. First are the Edmonton and Calgary, Alberta Jubilee auditoriums. These identical-twin buildings with 2700-seat fan-shaped auditoriums, were constructed simultaneously in the two cities. The architectural design was undertaken by the Architectural Branch of the Department of Public Works of Alberta. The second example is the Frederic R. Mann Auditorium in Tel

Aviv, built as the home of the Israel Philharmonic Orchestra and designed by architects, Rechter, Rechter and Karmi. The seating capacity is 2715, almost identical to the Calgary halls.

40 The Building Research Station was a government-funded research institute located at Garston, Watford to the north of London. Peter Parkin was an acoustician and William Allen was an architect with a keen interest in the subject.

41 John Summerson, 'Introduction', in John Summerson *45–55 Ten Years of British Architecture*, London, The Arts Council, 1956. Cited in John McKean, *Royal Festival Hall: Architecture in Detail*, London, Phaidon Press, 1992.

42 P.H. Parkin, W.A. Allen, H.J. Purkis and W.E. Scholes, 'The Acoustics of the Royal Festival Hall, London', *Acoustica*, Vol. 3, No. 1, 1953, pp. 1–21.

43 Hope Bagenal, 'Musical Taste and Concert Hall Design', *Proceedings of the Royal Musical Society*, 78th Sess., 1951–1952.

44 Bagenal had rejected the fan-shaped hall earlier when he was acoustics consultant for the auditorium of the Watford Town Hall that was completed in 1940. The architect was C.C. Voysey, son of the major architect of the Arts and Crafts movement, C.F.A. Voysey. The architectural language was described by Pevsner as, 'chaste neo-Georgian'. See Michael Barron, *Auditorium Acoustics and Architectural Design*, London, E. & F.N. Spon, 1993.

45 Michael Barron, *Auditorium Acoustics and Architectural Design*, op cit.

46 Ibid.

47 Ibid.

48 Lionel March, 'The Logic of Design and the Question of Value', op cit.

49 Dean Hawkes, 'Types, Norms and Habits in Environmental Design', in Lionel March (Ed.), *The Architecture of Form*, op cit.

50 In England, four halls built in the immediate post-war period may be regarded as direct progeny of the Royal Festival Hall. The Colston Hall in Bristol that replaced a hall destroyed by fire in 1945 also opened in 1951 with acoustics consultancy from the Building Research Station team, H.R. Humphreys, P.H. Parkin and William Allen, who collaborated with Hope Bagenal on the Festival Hall. The Free Trade Hall in Manchester was also a replacement for an earlier hall, this time destroyed during the Second World War. Hope Bagenal was, again, acoustic consultant. The Fairfield Hall in Croydon opened in 1962 and, as Barron observes, Hope Bagenal, as consultant, regarded the project as an opportunity to remedy the faults, which were by then perceived in the design of the Royal Festival Hall. This lineage continued with the opening of the Wessex Hall at Poole in Dorset, now with Peter Parkin as consultant. These halls are described and evaluated in detail by Michael Barron in *Auditorium Acoustics and Architectural Design*, op cit.

51 A review of the contribution of these architects is, Peter Blundell-Jones and Jian Kang, 'Acoustic Form and the Modern Movement', *Architectural Research Quarterly*, Vol. 7, No. 1, 2003, pp. 75–85.

52 Colin St John Wilson, *The Other Tradition of Modern Architecture: The Uncompleted Project*, London, Academy Editions, 1995.

53 Alvar Aalto, 'The Humanising of Architecture', *Technology Review*, 1940, reprinted in *Sketches: Alvar Aalto*, Göran Schildt (Ed.), Cambridge, MA, MIT Press, 1985.

54 See Dean Hawkes, 'The 'Other' Environmental Tradition: Nordic Masters', in Dean Hawkes *The Environmental Imagination: Technics and Poetics of the Architectural Environment*, London & New York, Routledge, 2nd Edition, 2019.

55 See Hans Girsberger and Karl Fleig (Eds.), *Alvar Aalto: The Complete Work, Volume 1*, Basel, Birkhäuser Verlag, 1963.

56 These diagrams may be found in Hans Girsberger and Karl Fleig (Eds.), *Alvar Aalto: The Complete Work*, Basel, Birkhäuser Verlag, Vol. 1, 1963, Vol. 2, 1971, Vol. 3, 1978.
57 Beranek, *Music Acoustics and Architecture*, op cit., reported favourably on the acoustics of Kultuuritalo, but Finlandia was less successful and Donna Cohen, 'Other Waves: The Acoustics of Alvar Aalto', *Proceedings of ACSA Annual Meeting and Technology Conference*, 1997, records the disagreement between Aalto and the acoustics consultant, Paavo Arni, on the validity of the architect's idea to construct and 'acoustically transparent' ceiling over the auditorium.
58 See Peter Blundell-Jones, *Hans Scharoun*, London, Phaidon Press, 1995 and Michael Barron, *Auditorium Acoustics and Architectural Design*, op cit.
59 Hans Scharoun, essay in *Berlin's Philharmonic Hall* (English edition), Berlin, Philharmonie, 1963.
60 Michael Barron, *Auditorium Acoustics and Architectural Design*, op cit.
61 Ibid.
62 Christopher Day, Harold Marshall, Thomas Scelo, Joanne Valentine and Peter Exton, 'The Philharmonie de Paris – Acoustic Design and Commissioning', Brisbane, *Proceedings of ACOUSTICS, 2016*.
63 Day, Marshall, et al., op cit, describe the entire design development in great detail. This involved extensive computer modelling using a range of architectural and acoustics software plus physical scale modelling of the acoustics.
64 This type is a reference to those halls, built mainly in the late nineteenth and early twentieth centuries, that were close to the form of conventional theatres, with proscenium stages and galleried auditoria.
65 Mike Barron, 'Developments in Concert Hall Acoustics in the 1960s: Theory and Practice', *Acoustics*, Vol. 1, 2019, pp. 538–548.
66 A.H. Marshall, 'A Note on the Importance of Room Cross-Section in Concert Halls', *Journal of the Acoustical Society of America*, Vol. 40, 1966, pp. 116–118. The idea of spatial responsiveness was further developed in, A.H. Marshall and M. Barron, 'Spatial Responsiveness in Concert Halls and the Origins of Spatial Impression', *Applied Acoustics*, Vol. 62, 2001, pp. 91–108.
67 Derek Sugden, *Cardiff Bay Opera House: Competition Brief*, Cardiff, Cardiff Bay Opera House Trust, 1994.
68 Among the 268 entries submitted, my own incorporated a horseshoe house within the body of the large overall form required by the brief, with generous foyers, restaurant, backstage facilities, administration and so on.
69 P.B. Medawar, 'Two Conceptions of Science', in P.B. Medawar, *The Art of the Soluble*, London, Methuen & Co., 1967.

Essay 11[1]
Musical affinities
Aalto and Kokkonen, Scarpa and Nono

Introduction

This essay follows from the visiting professorship that I held at the School of Architecture at the University of Huddersfield between 2002 and 2013. The School of Music at Huddersfield has an international reputation and each year organises the world-class Huddersfield Contemporary Music Festival. At their invitation, I gave a talk on the subject of 'Architecture and Music' during the Festival in 2003. For this I constructed 'digital essays' in which I juxtaposed images of buildings with recordings of musical works. In each case, the 'affinity' proposed was suggested by specific narrative and biographical links between the respective architects and composers. The subjects of the 'essays' are, first, Alvar Aalto (1898–1976) and Joonas Kokkonen (1921–1996) and, second, Carlo Scarpa (1906–1978) and Luigi Nono (1924–1990).

I begin with the statement, usually attributed to Johan Wolfgang von Goethe,[2]

> Architecture is frozen music.

The analogy between architecture and music is at first sight attractive, particularly with regard to questions of the formal organisation of both buildings and musical compositions. This is shown throughout the history of architecture from antiquity to the present day.

In his description of the design of 'The Theatre' in Book V, Ch. III, of The Ten Books on Architecture, Vitruvius wrote:

> Voice is a flowing breath of air, perceptible to the hearing by contact. It moves in an endless number of circular rounds, like the increasing circular waves which appear when a stone is thrown into smooth water. ... In the same manner the voice executes its movements in concentric circles; but while in the case of water the circles move horizontally on a plane surface, but also ascends vertically by regular stages. ... Hence the ancient architects, following in the footsteps of nature, perfected

DOI: 10.4324/9781003083023-12

the ascending rows of seats from their investigations of the ascending
voice, and, by means of the canonical theory of the mathematicians
and that of the musicians, endeavoured to make every voice uttered on
the stage come with greater clearness and sweetness to the ears of the
audience.[3]

Here a direct analogy is established between a theoretical statement on the
propagation of sound and the geometry of the ancient theatre. In the following chapter, Ch. IV, Vitruvius offers a detailed account of, 'Harmonics ... an
obscure and difficult branch of musical science.'[4]

The question of harmonic proportion was at the heart of the theoretical
debate in renaissance architecture and was explored at length by Wittkower
in, 'The Problem of Harmonic Proportion in Architecture'.[5] There, in a
series of analyses, he demonstrates the harmonic proportions in Palladio's
buildings. Writing of the Villa Malcontenta, he explains:

> The smallest room on either side of the cross-shaped hall measures
> twelve by sixteen feet, the next one sixteen by sixteen and the largest
> sixteen by twenty-four, while the width of the hall is thirty-two feet.
> Thus the consistent series, 12, 16, 24, 32 is the keynote to the building.
> As if in an overture the first and last members of this series appear in
> the ratio 12:32 of the portico, which is a diapason and a Diatessaron
> (i.e. 12:24:32).

Moving forward to the twentieth century, the British musicologist, Donald
Mitchell, drew a comparison, in *The Language of Modern Music*,[6] between
two giants of the respective arts, Le Corbusier and Arnold Schoenberg. He
begins with the following, at this point anonymous, quotation,

> I think one may claim that one of the main tasks that faced the crea-
> tors of the New Music was *reintegration*. Perhaps it might be expressed
> thus, this seeking after new means of composing, of putting together:
>   'To obtain the status of a rule: to uncover the principle capable of
> serving as a rule.'

Mitchell then reveals, 'Those words are not mine. They are not even the
words of a musician. They comprise, in fact, the definition of 'standardiza-
tion' by the architect Le Corbusier'.

In developing his argument, Mitchell illustrated the deep similarities
between Le Corbusier's *Le Modulor* and Schoenberg's 'Method of Composing
with Twelve Tones'.[7] The subtitle of *Le Modulor*, 'A Harmonious Measure
of the Human Scale Universally Applicable to Architecture and Mechanics'
is, it is suggested, analogous to the extended title of Schoenberg's essay,
'Method of Composing with Twelve Tones Which are Related Only with
One Another'. At this point in architectural and musical modernism,

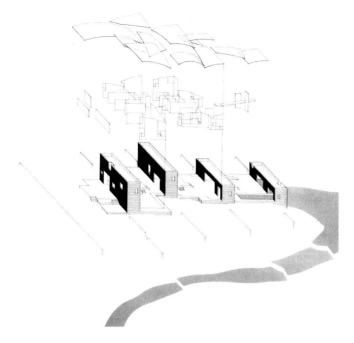

Figure 11.1 Steven Holl, Stretto House, Dallas, Texas. (Courtesy of Steven Holl)

architecture and music are claimed to share much methodological common ground.

A more overt connection was explored later in the twentieth century by Steven Holl with his design for the 'Stretto House' at Dallas, Texas, completed in 1992 (Figure 11.1).[8] 'Stretto' is a device in musical counterpoint in which the imitation of the subject in close succession is answered before it is completed. Holl suggested that a series of overlapping ponds on the site for the house were analogous to the effect of stretto and wrote, 'this dovetailing musical concept could, I imagined, be an idea for a fluid connection of architectural spaces'. His next step was to choose a musical work that uses stretto extensively, Béla Bartok's *Music for Strings, Percussion and Celesta, SZ 106, BB114*. Here he made an analogy between the music and the architecture of the house. 'In four movements, the piece has a distinct division between heavy (percussion) and light (strings). Where music has a materiality in instrumentation and sound, this architecture attempts an analog in light and space'.

The analogy is represented quite literally in the four movements of the music and the four separate structural and spatial blocks of the house and in the play between heavy structure, in the form of concrete blockwork – the 'percussion' of the building, and the light, curving steel structures of the roofs – the 'strings'.

Affinities: case studies

My aim in constructing the case studies, 'digital essays', that I presented at Huddersfield, was to explore less explicit possibilities of how architecture and music may come together. These derive from specific personal relationships between significant architects and composers of the twentieth century.

Aalto and Kokkonen

Alvar Aalto and Joonas Kokkonen were close friends. In discussing their relationship Louna Lahti records that Kokkonen was deeply touched by Aalto's view that, 'What is important in art is passion for quality, and only that.'[9] In 1967, the friendship was given concrete expression when Kokkonen commissioned Aalto to design a house on the shore of Lake Tusuula outside the town of Järvenpää, north of Helsinki (Figure 11.2). The town is a major locus in the musical life of Finland because Jean Sibelius (1865–1957), the country's most famous composer, lived there for over half a century, from 1904 until his death, at 'Ainola', a house designed for him by Lars Sonck (1870–1956), the great architect of the Finnish National Romantic movement.

In his lifetime, Joonas Kokkonen was considered to be Finland's preeminent composer, following the death of Sibelius. He wrote works in many

Figure 11.2 Alvar Aalto, Villa Kokkonen, Järvenpää. (Dean Hawkes)

forms and his four symphonies were regarded as the greatest body of works in the genre after those of Sibelius.[10] He was deeply interested in the idea of 'Finnishness' and its expression across the arts. He is recorded as stating that when he went to an old city, he would rather visit the medieval church than go to a concert because of his sensibility to shape.[11] He and Aalto met and became friends when, in 1963, Kokkonen was elected to the Finnish Academy, the nation's most distinguished cultural institution, of which Aalto was chairman.

Kokkonen recorded how the project for the house began when he telephoned Aalto to ask if there was an assistant in the office who might design a house for him. After a silence Aalto said, 'In principle I no longer design private houses, but I will do it for you!' On the day of the first visit to the site, Aalto and Kokkonen lunched at a restaurant in Järvenpää where, 'Alvar grabbed a pen from his pocket and drew a grand piano on the cloth. Then he asked me, "how do you move? Do you want to be able to walk round the piano?" I said, "Willingly!" Then he drew these lines for the study where the long side was a wavy line. And he said that if we wanted to be a little more inventive we could do so and so. In a very short time we had the floor plan.' Kokkonen further commented that 'The entire house has wonderful acoustics. It's like Finlandia Hall in miniature. They were designed at the same time you know.'[12] On the question of music and architecture, Kokkonen said, 'We talked a lot about the composer's work, but I never discovered Aalto's relationship with music. We talked about the similarities between music and architecture. For me, the architecture of music is very important. I'm unable to begin composing a new work if I don't know how it will end. I want a large work to have a solid form, it must be made from only a few elements. Alvar accepted that idea! The roof was originally the same as in Villa Mairea, but he came and re-designed it right here on the spot.'[13]

Situated across the lake from Sibelius' Ainola, Villa Kokkonen is an important example of Aalto's late work. The wonderfully lucid plan makes a clear distinction between the conventional apartments of a private house and the special conditions of the music room. The boundary between the two worlds has to provide a high level of sound insulation, a quite difficult technical problem in timber-frame construction, which was solved by using a double wall structure with a lead lining, to provide the mass necessary to reduce sound transmission, and a massive sliding door.

There is no literal, formal connection between Kokkonen's music and Aalto's architecture of the kind that was suggested by Steven Holl in his description of the Stretto House. Nonetheless, I suggest that the works of the two men share an affinity through common aspects of the arts in twentieth-century Finland. This hinges around the idea of the 'Other' tradition that was argued by Colin St John Wilson in relation to architecture[14] and which, I propose, has parallel developments in Finnish music.

According to Edward Jurkowski,[15] Finnish music was, for most of the early part of the twentieth century, dominated by, 'the shadow of Sibelius'.

Sibelius was undoubtedly Finland's foremost composer, and his music was cast in the Romantic tradition of the nineteenth century. The backbone of his output is the seven symphonies that date from 1899 to 1924. After that date, he entered what is referred to as 'the Järvenpää silence', 33 years when he lived at 'Ainola' and composed no new music. Jurkowski outlines the difficulty that younger Finnish composers experienced in the inter-war years, in exploring the new musical ideas that were emerging elsewhere in Europe, facing 'harsh criticism' from both critics and audiences.

Kokkonen's early compositions, spanning from the 1940s to the 50s, were post-romantic, 'spiced with some traits he had picked up from more recent European music.'[16] Then, in 1957, the year of Sibelius' death, Kokkonen adopted for the first time the dodecaphonic method of composition, using the twelve tones of the chromatic scale, that was devised in the 1920s by Arnold Schoenberg, thereby coming closer to one of the principal movements in twentieth-century music. A number of critics have suggested that he then moved on to his 'freely tonal' period that began with the composition of the third symphony in 1967. Jurkowski, however, goes to great lengths to demonstrate that, whilst Kokkonen's music did change in manner with this work, he continued to use the twelve-tone method, but in association with traditional devices, specifically triadic harmonies, that allowed him to harmonise the tone rows. Put simply, this allowed him to adapt the central method of musical modernism to wider expressive ends.

Kokkonen's *Cello Concerto* was the first work he composed in the new house. It directly addresses his relationship with Aalto and, through this, of architecture and music:

> 'Three people were immediately involved in the composition of this piece. It is dedicated to the architect Alvar Aalto, for this was the first major work which I completed in our new house, which Alvar designed. The dedication is not merely an expression of thanks for this great architectural master, however: when composing this concerto, I often remembered my extensive conversations with Alvar Aalto, which made me more aware than ever before of the close relationship between music and architecture – a relationship much deeper and richer than words can express'.[17]

The whole work has a lyrical quality that might be said to have parallels in the relationship between Aalto's architecture and that of the mainstream European modernists. Colin St John Wilson described Aalto's Villa Mairea (1937) as, 'the explicit weaving together of themes from Purism to traditional Karelian vernacular.'[18] Kokkonen dedicated the Adagio of the *Cello Concerto*, the third movement, to the memory of his mother and described it as, 'not a dirge, but the expression of light-filled memory overshadowed by longing'. In my sound and image presentation at Huddersfield, I chose the second movement, *Allegretto*, from the concerto, partly because of its brevity – three minutes – but principally because its delicacy and grace of manner seemed, described by Korhonen as, 'elegant, rolling, dancingly light, lucid and even playful at times'[19] to parallel the lyrical quality that is to be discovered in Aalto's architecture and, in particular, wonderfully apt to accompany the light-filled images of Villa Kokkonen that I captured on my visit on a beautiful autumn day in 2004.

Aalto heard the *Cello Concerto* at its premiere in a concert to celebrate Kokkonen's 50th birthday in Helsinki on 16 October 1969. Elisa Aalto, Alvar Aalto's second wife, said that this was the only piece of music he had listened to at a concert from start to finish. By most accounts, music did not play a central part in the architect's life. His daughter, Hanni, reported that her mother, Aino, 'played the piano almost every night and created such a soothing atmosphere ... And singing comforted her when she needed it. It was also a good thing for my father. He used to hum often, although he wasn't really musical. Sometimes the notes fell in the right place.'[20] Hanni also noted that, 'father was not actually very musical, but he could tinkle away on the piano and sing loudly or hum off-key, and sometimes he even hit the right note.'[21] Nonetheless, from the evidence of Kokkonen's accounts of his conversations with Aalto on the relationship between their respective arts and of the conception of the house, and from the experience of the concerto written in that wonderful studio, I propose that the two works are rooted in the same cultural soil of twentieth-century Finland.

Scarpa and Nono

Carlo Scarpa and Luigi Nono were both Venetians. Nono was a leading member of the European musical *avant-garde*, alongside such figures as Karlheinz Stockhausen, Pierre Boulez and Gyorgy Ligetti. His wife, Nuria, is the daughter of Arnold Schoenberg. The musician and the architect enjoyed a long friendship, the nature of which is discussed at length by Federica Goffi-Hamilton.[22] In 1955, Scarpa made a design for a work table for Nono and Nuria, as a wedding gift. This was made by the Venetian cabinet-maker, Saverio Anfodillo, and was used by Nono for the remainder of his life.[23]

The most eloquent expression of the relationship that existed between the two men is Nono's composition, *A Carlo Scarpa: architetto ai suoi infiniti possibili*. This is an intense work for a large orchestra of just under ten minutes duration, that was composed in 1984, six years after Scarpa's death. Martin Kaltennecker has described the piece as,

> a music which does not impose itself, but which is gently suggestive. Dedicated to a deceased architect friend, this hieratic work evokes sombre, sacred spaces, crossed by dark processions, a space for meditation and prayer. ... Events follow each other quickly at a minute level with allegros of timbre and miniscule variations. But these involve perception

through adjusting our sense of hearing in a different way; this in the final analysis is the social stake in an aesthetic protesting against the contemporary world.[24]

Nono's music is immensely complex in form, organisation and sonority, but Kaltenecker points out that it is derived from an 'invention upon two notes (C and E flat)'. In German musical notation, E flat is given as Es (S). The two fundamental notes of the composition become, therefore, Scarpa's initials – CS. Elaborating on the significance of Nono's dedication, Nicolaus A. Huber writes that it gives, 'the impression of cosmically scattered fragments of sonic material; of a musical chain of terse or even coarse and leaden sound blocks, separated from one another by various pauses. Only after some reflection can one recognise the differentiations and dispersals that go with them, as well as the *infinite possibilities*'.[25]

Huber also shows that the organisation of the sonic material of the work is based on the Fibonacci series. This follows the principle below:

3 woodwind colours (4 flutes, 3 piccolos, 3 clarinets, 3 bassoons)
3 brass colours (3 trumpets, 4 horns, 4 trombones) and
4 string colours (made up of 8 violins, violas, cellos, double bass)
adding up to a total of **10**.
In addition, there is a percussion group of **4** colours
(celesta, harp, 2 tubular bells, 2 timpani) and **7** different pitched triangles,
adding up to a total of **11**.
This gives a central order based on the Fibonacci number **21**:
3+3+4=10, 4+7=11. 10+11=21

Is it possible that the adoption of a 'geometrical' system could be a cipher for the architecture of the composer's friend? In writing about his design for the Brion cemetery at San Vito d'Altivole, which was to become the site of his own tomb, Scarpa described how,

everything (is) on a grid of 5.5 centimetres. This motif which seems nothing special is actually rich in expressive scope and movement ... I measured everything with the numbers 11 and 5.5. Since everything was based on multiplication, everything fits and all the measurements turned out right ... Many architects use regulatory plans or the golden section. Mine is a very simple grid which allows for movement – the centimetre is arid, while in my way you obtain a relationship.[26]

The appearance of the number 11 in both the instrumentation of Nono's music and Scarpa's design is intriguing, but almost certainly a question of coincidence rather than of shared method. Marco Frascari explored this numerical theme in Scarpa's work more widely in his essay, 'Architectural Traces of an Admirable Cipher: Eleven in the Opus of Carlo Scarpa'.[27]

The choice of a building to combine with Nono's music for my audio-visual presentation was, for me, easily decided. At first sight it might seem most appropriate to select the Brion cemetery, where Scarpa is buried and at which he applied his 'wonderful cipher' on the number 11 – coincidentally – or is it not coincidence? – the total of percussion instruments in Nono's musical tribute. But Kaltenecker's reference to 'sombre, sacred spaces, crossed by dark processions', brought immediately to my mind the extension to the Museo Canoviano at Possagno (Figure 11.3), a building I have visited many times, whose spaces, with their ever-changing light and shade evoke, for me, a strong sense of the sombre and sacred.[28] The analogy of light and sound seems particularly apt in the case of Scarpa and Nono. Boris Podrecca's description of the light of Scarpa's buildings is eloquent:

> it is not just the physical presence of things that transfigures tradition, but also the light, which is a *lumen* not of tomorrow but of the past – the light of the golden background, of the glimmering liquid, of the ivory-coloured inlay, of luminous and shimmering fabrics recreated in marble. It is the light of a reflection of the world.[29]

Figure 11.3 Carlo Scarpa, Museo Canoviano, Possagno, Detail. (Gerry Johansson)

The building, on which Scarpa began work in 1955, is an addition to the nineteenth-century neo-classical basilican gallery by Francesco Lazzari on the grounds of Antonio Canova's house at Possagno. In contrast to the formal display in Lazzari's gallery, Scarpa's totally different 'free' composition of volumes sets Canova's exquisite plaster figures within an ever-changing field of light that, as Sergio Los has written, 'pours in – at times with glaring violence, at other times softly and faintly … modifying them over the course of the day, with the changing seasons and the variations in the weather'.[30] I find this vivid description of the temporal, visual experience of the building, particularly the references to 'glaring violence' and 'softly and faintly' to strongly parallel the sonic experience of Nono's music.

Coda

In exploring these connections between architecture and music, my aim has been to add a little to the wider understanding of twentieth-century culture. In particular to show how significant practitioners have, through intellectual affinities and acts of friendship and regard, added to the literature of their respective arts. The architectural and musical worlds of Aalto and Kokkonen are quite different from those of Scarpa and Nono, although they share in the same spirit of adventure and experiment that characterised the arts of the century in which they all lived and worked. My intention in undertaking these studies was to add a small new perspective on the arts of this period.

Discography

Case 1

Alvar Aalto: Villa Kokkonen, Järvenpää, Finland, 1967–1969.
Joonas Kokkonen: *Cello Concerto*, 1969.
Recording: Arto Noras, Cello, Helsinki Philharmonic Orchestra, conductor Paul Freeman, Finlandia Records, 1979.

Case 2

Carlo Scarpa: Museo Canoviano, Possagno, 1955–1957.
Luigi Nono: *A Carlo Scarpa: architetto ai suoi infiniti possibili*, 1984.
Recording: Orchester des Südwestfunks, conductor Michael Gielen, Audivis/Naïve, 2000.

Notes

1 This essay derives from a talk given at the Huddersfield Contemporary Music Festival in 2003 and is a revised version of an essay first published in *Scroope: Cambridge Architecture Journal*, No. 18, 2004, with the title, 'Thawing Goethe: Musical Connections'.

2 In a letter to Johann Peter Eckermann, dated 23rd March 1929, Goethe wrote, 'I call architecture frozen music'. However, this was anticipated by over 20 years by Friedrich von Schelling who, in *Philosophie der Kunst*, 1802–1803, stated, 'Architecture in general is frozen music'.

3 Vitruvius, *The Ten Books on Architecture*, Book V, Chapter III, 6 – 8, M.H. Hickey Morgan (trans), New York, Dover Books, 1060.

4 Vitruvius, op cit., Book V, Chapter, IV.

5 Rudolph Wittkower, 'The Problem of Harmonic Proportion in Architecture', in Rudolph Wittkower, *Architectural Principles in the Age of Humanism*, 5th Edition, London, Academy Editions, 1998.

6 Donald Mitchell, *The Language of Modern Music*, London, Faber & Faber, 1963.

7 The first French editions of *Le Modulor* were published in 1950 and 1955 and the English translation *The Modulor*, in 1954, London, Faber & Faber. Schoenberg's 'Method of Composing with Twelve Tones Which are Related Only with One Another' was first presented as a lecture in 1940 and published in Arnold Schoenberg, *Style and Idea*, New York, Philosophical Library, 1950.

8 Steven Holl, *The Stretto House*, New York, Monacelli Press, 1996.

9 Louna Lahti, 'Of Music and Architecture', *Finnish Music Quarterly*, Vol. 1, 2004, pp. 24–29.

10 Edward Jurkowski, *The Music of Joonas Kokkonen*, Farnham, Ashgate, 2004, reissued London & New York, Routledge, 2018.

11 Kokkonen in conversation with Jeffrey Richard Sandborg, *Modern Finnish Choral Music and Joonas Kokkonen's 'Requiem'*, D.Mus. Arts thesis, University of Illinois, 1991 (unpublished).

12 Interview with Joonas Kokkonen in Louna Lahti, *Alvar Aalto: Ex Intimo*, Helsinki, Rakennustieto, 2001.

13 Ibid.

14 Colin St John Wilson, *The Other Tradition of Modern Architecture: The Uncompleted Project*, London, Academy Editions, 1995.

15 Edward Jurkowski, *The Music of Joonas Kokkonen*, op cit.

16 Joonas Kokkonen, cited by Kimmo Korhonen, liner notes to CD recording, *Meet the Composer: Joonas Kokkonen*, Finlandia Records, 1996.

17 Joonas Kokkonen quoted in Edward Jurkowski, *The Music of Joonas Kokkonen*, op cit.

18 Colin St John Wilson, *The Other Tradition of Modern Architecture*, op cit.

19 Kimmo Korhonen, liner notes to CD recording, op cit.

20 Interview with Hanni Alanen (Aalto) in Louna Lahti, *Alvar Aalto: Ex Intimo*, op cit.

21 Louna Lahti, 'Of Music and Architecture', op cit.

22 Federica Goffi-Hamilton, 'Carlo Scarpa and the Eternal Canvas of Silence', *Architectural Research Quarterly*, Vol. 10, No. 3/4, 2006, pp. 291–300.

23 The table is illustrated by Goffi-Hamilton, ibid, in three images, one showing the table in Nono's 'working space' at the time he was composing his work in memory of Scarpa, the second a detail of the leg of the table which is juxtaposed with a reproduction of Scarpa's drawing of the same detail.

24 Martin Kaltenecker, liner notes to CD recording of *A Carlo Scarpa: architetto ai suoi possibili infiniti*, Audivis Naïve, 2000.

25 Nicolaus A. Huber, 'Nuclei and Dispersal in Luigi Nono's *A Carlo Scarpa: architetto ai suoi infiniti possibili* per orchestra a microintervalli, in 'Luigi Nono: Fragments and Silence (1924–1990), *Contemporary Music Review*, Vol. 18, Part 2, 1999.

26 Carlo Scarpa, 'A Thousand Cypresses', lecture given in Madrid, 1978, reprinted in Francesco Dal Co and Giuseppe Mazzariol (Eds.), *Carlo Scarpa: The Complete Works*, English edition, London, Electa/The Architectural Press, 1984.

27 Marco Frascari, 'Architectural Traces of an Admirable Cipher: In the Opus of Carlo Scarpa', *Nexus Network Journal*, Vol. 1, 1999, pp. 7–21. This is an extended version of an earlier essay, 'A Deciphering of a Wonderful Cipher: Eleven in the Architecture of Carlo Scarpa', in *Oz 13*, 1991.

28 See Essay 5: Carlo Scarpa: 'I Wish I Could Frame the Blue of the Sky', in Dean Hawkes (Ed.), *The Environmental Imagination: Technics and Poetics of the Environmental Imagination*, London, Routledge, 2nd edition, 2019, for my analysis of the experience of this building.

29 Boris Podrecca, 'A Viennese Point of View', in Francesco Dal Co and Giuseppe Mazzariol (Eds.), *Carlo Scarpa: The Complete Works*, Milan, Electa/London, The Architectural Press, 1986.

30 Sergio Los, 'Carlo Scarpa – Architect and Poet', in *Ptah: Architecture Design Art*, Helsinki, 2001:2, pp. 30–38.

Bibliography

This presents the principal books that are referred to in the text. References to essays, articles and other sources are given in full in the Notes to each essay.

Alexander, Christopher, *Notes on the Synthesis of Form*, Cambridge, MA, Harvard University Press, 1967.

Bagenal, Hope and Alex Wood, *Designing for Good Acoustics*, London, Methuen & Co, 1931.

Banham, Reyner, *The Architecture of the Well-tempered Environment*, London, The Architectural Press, 1969, 2nd Edition, Chicago, University of Chicago Press, 1984.

Barron, Michael, *Auditorium Acoustics and Architectural Design*, London, E& FN Spon, 1993.

Bennett, J.A., *The Mathematical Sciences of Christopher Wren*, Cambridge, UK, Cambridge University Press, 1982.

Benton, Tim and Charlotte with Dennis Sharp, *From and Function: A Sourcebook for the History of Architecture and Design 1890–1939*, London, Granada Publishing Ltd., 1975.

Beranek, Leo L., *Music, Acoustics and Architecture*, New York & London, John Wiley & Son, 1962.

Blundell-Jones, Peter, *Hans Scharoun*, London, Phaidon Press, 1995.

Boynton, Lindsay (Ed.), *The Hardwick Hall Inventory of 1601*, London, The Furniture History Society, 1971.

Campbell, Colen, *Vitruvius Britannicus*, London, Vols. 1–3, 1715, 1717, 1725.

Chambers, William, *A Treatise on the Decorative Part of Civil Architecture*, London, 1759.

Chermayeff, Serge and Christopher Alexander, *Community and Privacy: Towards a New Architecture of Humanism*, New York, Doubleday & Co., 1963, Harmondsworth, Pelican Books, 1966.

Chorley, Richard and Peter Haggett, (Eds.), *Models in Geography*, London, Methuen & Co., 1967.

Clarke, David, *Analytical Archaeology*, London, Methuen & Co., 1968.

Colquhoun, Alan, *Essays in Architectural Criticism*, Cambridge, MA, MIT Press, 1985.

Craft, Robert, *Conversations with Igor Stravinsky*, London, Faber and Faber Ltd., 1959.

Dal Co, Francesco and Giuseppe Mazzariol (Eds.), *Carlo Scarpa: The Complete Works*, English Edition, London, The Architectural Press, 1986.

Dini, M., *Renzo Piano: Projects and Buildings 1964–1983*, London, Electa/The Architectural Press, 1985.

Downes, Kerry, *A Thousand Years of the Church of St. Stephen Walbrook*, London, St. Stephens Walbrook, undated.

Durant, David N., *Bess of Hardwick: Portrait of an Elizabethan Dynast*, Revised Edition, London, Peter Owen Publishers, 1999.

Durant, David N., *The Smythson Circle: The Story of Six Great English Houses*, London, Peter Owen Publishers, 2011.

Durant, David N. and Philip Riden, *The Building of Hardwick Hall, Part 1, 1587-1591: The Old Hall, Part 2, The New Hall, 1591–1598*, Chesterfield, Derbyshire Record Society, Vol. 4, 1980, Vol. 9, 1984.

Fagan, Brian, *The Little Ice Age: How Climate Made History*, New York, Basic Books, 2002.

Fleckner, Sigurd, *Reichsforschungsgesellschaft für Wirtschaftlichkeit in Bau und Wohnungswesen*, Aachen, RWTH Publications, 1993.

Forsyth, Michael, *Buildings for Music: The Architect, the Musician, and the Listener from the Seventeenth Century to the Present Day*, Cambridge, UK, Cambridge University Press, 1985.

Foster, Hal (Ed.), *Postmodern Culture*, London & Concord, MA, Pluto Press, 1983.

Frampton, Kenneth, *Studies in Tectonic Culture: the Poetics of Construction in Nineteenth and Twentieth Century Architecture*, Cambridge, MA, MIT Press, 1995.

Friedman, Alice T., *House and Household in Elizabethan England: Wollaton Hall and the Willoughby Family*, Chicago, University of Chicago Press, 1989.

Gale, Matthew and Chris Stephens, *Francis Bacon*, exhibition catalogue, London, Tate Publishing, 2008.

Giedion, Sigfried, *Mechanization Takes Command: A Contribution to Anonymous History*, Oxford, Oxford University Press, 1948.

Girsberger, Hans and Karl Fleig (Eds.), *Alvar Aalto: The Complete Work, Volume 1*, Basel, Birkhäuser Verlag, Vol. 1, 1963, Vol. 2, 1971, Vol. 3, 1978.

Girouard, Mark, *Robert Smythson and the English Country House*, New Haven, CT & London, Yale University Press, 1983.

Gropius, Walter, *The New Architecture and the Bauhaus*, London, Faber & Faber, 1935.

Gwilt, Joseph, *An Encyclopaedia of Architecture: Historical, Theoretical and Practical*, 1st Edition, London, Longmans, Brown & Green, 1825.

Hawkes, Dean, *The Environmental Tradition*, London, & New York, E & FN Spon, 1996.

Hawkes, Dean, *The Environmental Imagination*, London & New York, Routledge, 2008, 2nd Edition, 2020.

Hawkes, Dean, *Architecture and Climate*, London & New York, Routledge, 2012.

Hertzberger, Herman, *Lessons for Students in Architecture*, Rotterdam, Uitgeverij 010 Publishers, 1991.

Hesse, Mary, *Models and Analogies in Science*, Indiana, University of Notre Dame Press, 1966.

Holl, Steven, *The Stretto House*, New York, Monacelli Press, 1996.

Hopkinson, R.G., *Architectural Physics: Lighting*, London, HMSO, 1964.

Humphrey, Michael, Fergus Nicol and Susan Roaf, *Adaptive Thermal Comfort: Foundations and Analysis*, Abingdon & New York, 2020.

Hunt, Frederick V., *Origins in Acoustics: The Science of Sound from Antiquity to the Age of Newton*, New Haven, Yale University Press, 1978.

Jardine, Lisa, *On a Grander Scale: The Outstanding Career of Christopher Wren*, London, Harper Collins, 2002.

Jeffrey, Paul, *The City Churches of Sir Christopher Wren*, London, Hambledon Continuum, 1996.

Jurkowski, Edward, *The Music of Joonas Kokkonen*, Farnham, Ashgate, 2004, reissued, London & New York, Routledge, 2018.

Knowles Middleton, W.E., *Invention of the Meteorological Instruments*, Baltimore, The Johns Hopkins Press, 1969.

Kuhn, Thomas, *The Structure of Scientific Revolutions*, Chicago, IL and London, University of Chicago Press, 1970.

Lahti, Louna, *Alvar Aalto: Ex Intimo*, Helsinki, Rakennustieto, 2001.

Langhans, Friedrich, *Ueber Theater*, Berlin, Gottfried Hayn, 1810.

Latham, Ian and Mark Swennarton (Eds.), *Feilden Clegg Bradley: The Environmental Handbook*, London, Right Angle Publishing, 2007.

Latour, Alexandra (Ed.), *Louis I. Kahn: Writings, Lectures, Interviews*, New York, Rizzoli International, 1991.

Lawrence, Ranald, *The Victorian Art School: Architecture, History and Environment*, Abingdon & New York, Routledge, 2020.

Le Corbusier, *Precisions on the Present State of Architecture and the City*, Paris, Crès et Cie, 1930, English Translation, Boston, MA, MIT Press, 1991.

Lea, F.M., *Science and Building: A History of the Building Research Station*, London, HMSO, 1971.

Lefaivre, Lianne and Alexander Tzonis, *Critical Regionalism: Architecture and Identity in a Globalized World*, Munich & London, Prestel, 2003.

Leoni, Giacomo, *The Architecture of Andrea Palladio in Four Books*, London, 1715.

Lethaby, W.R., *Architecture: An Introduction to the History and Theory of the Art of Building*, London, Thornton Butterworth Ltd., 1911.

Macleod, Robert, *Style and Society: Architectural Ideology in Britain 1835-1914*, London, RIBA Publications, 1971

March, Lionel (Ed.), *The Architecture of Form*, Cambridge, UK, Cambridge University Press, 1976.

Marshall, Pamela, *Wollaton Hall: An Archaeological Survey*, Nottingham, Nottingham Civic Society, 1996.

Martin, Leslie, *Buildings and Ideas 1933–1983: From the Studio of Leslie Martin and His Associates*, Cambridge, UK, Cambridge University Press, 1983.

Martin, Leslie and Colin Buchanan, *Whitehall: A Plan for the National and Government Centre*, London, HMSO, 1965.

Martin, Leslie and Lionel March (Eds.), *Urban Space and Structures*, Cambridge, UK, Cambridge University Press, 1972.

Mason, Richard (Ed.), *Cambridge Minds*, Cambridge, Cambridge University Press, 1994.

Martin, Leslie, Ben Nicholson and Naum Gabo (Eds.), *Circle International Survey of Constructive Art*, London, Faber & Faber, 1937, reprinted 1971.

McKean, John, *Royal Festival Hall: Architecture in Detail*, London, Phaidon Press, 1992.

Medawar, P.B., *The Art of the Soluble*, London, Methuen, 1967.

Mitchell, Donald, *The Language of Modern Music*, London, Faber & Faber, 1963.

Morris, Robert, *An Essay in Defence of Ancient Architecture*, London, 1728.

Morris, Robert, *Lectures on Architecture*, London, J. Brindley, 2 Vols, 1734–1736.

Morris, Robert, *Rural Architecture*, London, 1750.

Morris, Robert, *Architectural Remembrancer*, London, 1751.

Mumford, Lewis, *Technics and Civilization*, London, Routledge, 1934.

Nicol, Fergus, Michael Humphrey and Susan Roaf, *Adaptive Thermal Comfort: Principles and Practice*, Abingdon & New York, Routledge, 2012.

Olgyay, Victor, *Design with Climate: Bioclimatic Approach to Architectural Regionalism*, Princeton, NJ, Princeton University Press, 1963, 2nd Edition, 2017.

Park, Katherine and Lorraine Daston (Eds.), *The Cambridge History of Science, Volume 3, Early Modern Science*, Cambridge, Cambridge University Press, 2006.

Parkin, P.H. and H.R. Humphries, *Acoustics, Noise and Building*, 1st Edition, London, Faber & Faber, 1958.

Palladio, Andrea, *I Quattro Libri dell'Architettura*, Venice, 1580.

Pevsner, Nikolaus, *Pioneers of Modern Design: from William Morris to Walter Gropius*, first published as *Pioneers of the Modern Movement*, London, Faber & Faber, 1936, revised edition, Harmondsworth, Penguin Books, 1960.

Pevsner, Nikolaus, *The Buildings of England: South Lancashire*, Harmondsworth, Penguin Books, 1969,

Plot, Robert, *The Natural History of Oxfordshire*, Oxford, printed at the Theatre, 1667.

Powers, Alan, *Serge Chermayeff: Designer, Architect, Teacher*, London, RIBA Publications, 2001.

Ronner, Heinz and Sharad Jhaveri, *Louis I. Kahn: Complete Works*, Basel, Birkhäuser, 1987.

Saunders, George, *Treatise on Theatres*, London, The Architectural Library, 1780.

Sabine, Wallace Clement, *Collected Papers on Acoustics*, Cambridge, MA, Harvard University Press, 1922. Reprinted edition, with introduction by Frederick V. Hunt, New York, Dover Publications, 1964.

Schoenberg, Arnold, *Style and Idea*, New York, Philosophical Library, 1950.

Schildt, Gōran (Ed.), *Sketches: Alvar Aalto*, Cambridge, MA, MIT Press, 1985.

Scott, Geffrey, *The Architecture of Humanism*, London, Constable & Co., 1914.

Sharples, Joseph, (Ed.), *Charles Reilly and the Liverpool of Architecture 1904–1933*, Liverpool, Liverpool University Press, 1996.

Smith, Bruce R. (Ed.), *The Cambridge Guide to the Worlds of Shakespeare*, Cambridge, Cambridge University Press, 2016.

Smithson, Peter, *Conversations with Students: A Space for our Generation*, Princeton, NJ, Princeton University Press, 2005.

Stravinsky, Igor, *Poetics of Music: In the Form of Six Lessons*, Cambridge, MA, Harvard University Press, 1942.

Stone, Richard, *Mathematics in the Social Sciences and Other Essays*, London, Chapman & Hall, 1966.

Summerson, John, *Heavenly Mansions and Other Essays on Architecture*, London, Cresset Press, 1949.

Summerson, John, *The Sheldonian in its Time*, Oxford, The Clarendon Press, 1964.

Summerson, John, *Architecture in Britain 1530-1830*, Harmondsworth, Penguin Books, 1969.

Summerson, John, *The Unromantic Castle and Other Essays*, London & New York, Thames & Hudson, 1990.

Thompson, Emily, *The Soundscape of Modernity: Architectural Acoustics and the Culture of Listening in America, 1900–1933*, Cambridge, MA, MIT Press, 2002.

Thornton, Peter, *Seventeenth-Century Interior Decoration in England*, France and Holland, New Haven, CT & London, Yale University Press, 1891.

Tzonis, Alexander, Lianne Lefaivre and Bruno Stagno, *Tropical Architecture: Critical Regionalism in the Age of Globalisation*, Chichester, Wiley-Academy, 2001.

Tzonis, Alexander and Lianne Lefaivre, *Architecture of Regionalism in the Age of Globalization*, London & New York, Routledge, 2012, 2nd edition, 2020.

Venturi, Robert, Denise Scott Brown and Stephen Izenour, *Learning from Las Vegas*, Cambridge, MA, MIT Press, 1972.

Vitruvius, *The Ten Books of Architecture*, (Trans.) W.H. Morgan, New York, Dover Books, 1960.

Watkin, David (Ed.), *Sir John Soane: The Royal Academy Lectures*, Cambridge, Cambridge University Press, 2000.

Whitehead, Alfred North, *The Function of Reason*, Princeton, NJ, Princeton University Press, 1929.

Wilkes, Maurice V., *Memories of a Computer Pioneer*, Cambridge, MA, MIT Press, 1985.

Wilson, Colin St John, *The Other Tradition of Modern Architecture: The Uncompleted Project*, London, Academy Editions, 1995.

Wittkower, Rudolph, *Architectural Principles in the Age of Humanism*, 5th Edition, London, Academy Editions, 1998.

Wood, Alex, *The Physical Basis of Music*, Cambridge, UK, Cambridge University Press, 1913.

Zumthor, Peter, *Thinking Architecture*, Basel, Boston, MA & Berlin, Birkhäuser – Publishers for Architecture, 1996.

Index

Page numbers in italics denote figures. Notes indicated by (page number) 'n'

McKim, Mead and White: Boston
Music Hall (Symphony Hall) 6, 130,
131, 132, 133, 136, 147
Medawar, P.B.: *The Art of the
Soluble* 10, 13n9, 39, 43, 44n18,
148, 152n69
Mendelsohn, Erich 24
Messina, Antonello da 19
Meunier, John 25
Mitchell, Donald: *The Language of
Modern Music* 154, 163n6
Morris, Robert 4, 72; *Lectures on
Architecture* 72, 79n46, 79n49
Mumford, Lewis: *Technics and
Civilization* 76n2
Murcutt, Glenn 112n22; Arthur and
Yvonne Boyd Art Centre, Riverdale,
NSW, Australia 105, *105*

Newton, Isaac 4, 61
Nicholson, Ben 24, 34n2, 36
Nono, Luigi 6, 153, 159; *Ai Carlo
Scarpa: architetto, ai suoi infiniti
possibili* 159, 162
Nouvel, Jean: DR Konserthuset,
Copenhagen 142; Philharmonie de
Paris 142, *142*

Olgyay, Victor 4; *Design with
Climate: Bioclimatic Approach to
Architectural Regionalism* 7n4, 92,
111n4, 112n13
Orlowski, Raf 148n4
Ott, Carlos: Opéra Bastille, Paris 145
Oxford Conference on Architectural
Education 2, 8–12, 13n4, 22, 23n8,
27, 35n9, 39, 42, 43n3

Palladio, Andrea 57, 62, 63; *I Quattro
Libri dell'Architettura* 72–74, 77n18,
79n45; Villa Capra (La Rotonda) 57,
62, 63; Villa Malcontenta 3, 75, 76
Parkin, P.H. 137, 148n4,
151n42, 151n50
Parkin, P.H. and H.R. Humphries
45; *Acoustics, Noise and Buildings*
125, 148n2
Patkau Architects: Strawberry Vale
Elementary School, Victoria, British
Columbia 103, *103*
Patte, Pierre: *Essai sur l'architecture
théâtrale* 127
Pevsner, Nikolaus 136, 150n37;
Pioneers of Modern Design 124n8

Piano, Renzo 124n13
Piano, Renzo and Richard Rogers:
Centre Pompidou, Paris 119, *120*
Piermarini, Giuseppe: La Scala, Milan
128, *128*, 149n2
Plot, Robert: *The Natural History of
Oxfordshire* 69, 78n35
Powers, Alan 32; *Serge Chermayeff:
Designer, Architect, Teacher* 35n186

Richards, I.A. 15, 23n6
Richter, Hans 130
Riden, Philip 58n2, 159n9
Rietveld, Gerrit: Schroeder House,
Utrecht 85
Rome, The Pantheon 95, *96*, 99
Rowe, Colin 38
Rowse, Herbert J.: Philharmonic Hall,
Liverpool 136, 150n38
Royal Society of London 61, 67,
69, 72
Rural Urban Framework: The Ger
Innovation Hub, Ulaanbaatar,
Mongolia 107, *107*
Ruskin, John 115–117

Saarinen, Eliel: Kleinhans Music Hall,
Buffalo 136
Sabine, Wallace Clement 5, 6, 130–133,
136, 141, 143, 147, 148, 149nn20–21,
150n26; *Collected Papers on
Acoustics* 7n8
Saunders, George 127; *Treatise on
Theatres* 149n16
Scamozzi, Vincenzo 127
Scarpa, Carlo iii, 2, 4–6, 19–21,
84, 85, 124n17, 153, 159, 160,
163n22–26, 164nn27–30; Brion
Cemetery, San Vito d'Altivole 160,
161; Castelvecchio, Verona *122*, 123;
Museo Canoviano, Possagno 4, 6,
85, 161, *161*, 162
Scharoun, Hans 6, 139, 147;
Philharmonie, Berlin 6, 140, *141*
Schoenberg, Arnold 154, 158,
159, 163n7
Scott, Geoffrey 5, 117, 119; *The
Architecture of Humanism* 7n5,
115, 124n4
Scott Brown, Denise 124n15
Scully, Vincent 99, 112n12, 120, 124n7
Selva, Giannnantonio: La Fenice,
Venice 126
Semper, Gottfried 129